MW00484006

Stay with God

STAY WITH GOD

A statement in illusion on Reality

Francis Brabazon

Illustrated by John Parry

N·B

New Humanity Books

STAY WITH GOD

A statement in illusion on Reality

by Francis Brabazon

Copyright © Avatar's Abode Trust 1984

All Rights Reserved

NEW HUMANITY BOOKS
83 Bourke Street
Melbourne Victoria 3000
AUSTRALIA

First Edition 1959

Second Edition 1977

Third Edition
First Illustrated Edition 1990

Paperback

ISBN 0 949191 07 8

Limited Edition 500 Cloth Copies
Published for
AVATAR FOUNDATION

Printed in Hong Kong by Bookbuilders

Francis Brabazon – A Biographical Sketch

Francis Brabazon was born in England in 1907. He moved to Australia with his family when he was a young child, the youngest of five children. They settled on a farm in Victoria. In his book THE WIND OF THE WORD he describes these early days. He was close to his father who had been a drama critic and through him became interested in literature. By his early teens he became disillusioned with his Anglican faith because of the lack of answers to his questions.

In the early 1930s in Melbourne, in the midst of the Depression, he worked at odd jobs and educated himself, learned to play the piano and achieved an unofficial Australian record at weightlifting. Francis met the Baron von Frankenburg, a Sufi teacher from the school of Hazrat Inayat Khan. Many of the Baron's group later became followers of the Spiritual Master Meher Baba. Francis began to paint, was drafted into the army early in the war but did not fit into the military life – too many questions again. An exhibition of his paintings in Melbourne during this period influenced the fledgling Antipodean Movement in Australian painting and especially the early work of one of Australia's greatest artists, Sidney Nolan.

Brabazon turned to poetry and was published in the controversial Angry Penguins Magazine and Ern Malley's Journal until his poetry became mystical and from then until his death was ignored by the various literary movements in Australia, except for the young La Mama poets of the late sixties. His first published books PROLETARIANS – TRANSITION and EARLY POEMS were written during the 1940s.

In 1947 the Baron gave Francis the DISCOURSES of Meher Baba. Meher Baba stated that he was the Avatar, the Christ, God in human form. Francis was extremely interested. The Baron died in 1950 and in 1952 Brabazon travelled to the USA and met Meher Baba, who made a profound impression upon him. In 1954 Meher Baba called Brabazon to India where they travelled to Andhra Pardesh. JOURNEY WITH GOD published in the same year describes this experience. SEVEN STARS TO MORNING, his first major book of poems was published in 1956, the year of Meher Baba's first visit to Australia. Country Life said of it: "... covers the planet in a riot of intellectual experience... sincerity and much dignity." This was followed by publication of a long narrative poem CANTOS OF WANDERING in 1957 and a book of seven mystical plays SINGING THRESHOLD in 1958. In the same year Meher Baba visited Australia again and stayed at a place in Woombye, Queensland, that Francis and other followers had built for him. This was to become known as Avatar's Abode.

Subsequent to this visit Meher Baba invited Francis to India again where he stayed with him as an intimate disciple for the following ten years until Meher Baba dropped his physical form in 1969. When Brabazon went to India he took with him the almost complete manuscript of STAY WITH GOD which Meher Baba had asked him to write. Francis says in the preface to a later work THE WORD AT WORLD'S END: "... I have infinitely crafted my ideas before beginning to write; and in my best work the idea forged its own form of expression. In STAY WITH GOD the opening line came to me twelve years before I wrote that book. And it was not an odd line jotted down and forgotten; I carried it with me, noting its possibilities and acquiring the material it would need." Meher Baba had the book read to him three times stating that it gave life to his own book GOD SPEAKS and said: "My love will touch the hearts of all who read it as no book has ever done."

STAY WITH GOD (1959) is a lucid exposition of the Advent on earth, in our time, of the God-Man and of this living embodiment of Godhood as the Salvation of Mankind from its state of permanent anxiety and threatened annihilation. This God-Man is not seen as the Son of a Father, but as the very Self of each one of us and therefore, easily knowable to anyone directly, without an intermediary. In the creative process of perceiving the meaning of the God-Man, the author examines the values of Mankind, both Eastern and Western, past and present, as represented in Art and Literature. His language, arising directly from the urgency of his message and the clarity of his vision, avoids rigid crystallizations, by which modern poetry is immobilized and essence and vitality excluded.

Upon return to Australia THE WORD AT WORLD'S END (1971) was published, then IN DUST I SING (1974), a collection of poems written at the insistence of Meher Baba. These poems were based on the form of the 'ghazal' – perfected by the Persian poet Hafiz of Shiraz (1320-1390): Meher Baba's favourite form of poetry. Another collection of Brabazon's 'ghazals', THE BELOVED IS ALL IN ALL, were published posthumously in 1988. Other published works of Francis Brabazon include LET US THE PEOPLE SING (1962) songs, THE EAST–WEST GATHERING (1963), THREE TALKS (1969), WIND OF THE WORLD (1976), THE SILENT WORD (1978) a biography of the early life of Meher Baba and THE GOLDEN BOOK OF PRAISE (1982), songs. Some of his writing remains unedited and unpublished. Francis Brabazon died in 1984. His grave is at Avatar's Abode on the side of the hill, under the pine trees, overlooking the ocean.

Preface

In this book I have tried to offer some praise to one who has not so much "changed the course of my life" as given it sanction. For the course of my life was already set when, as a child, I used to weep at the beauty of night; and a little later on compose verses on the "meaning of life" as I walked behind the plough.

The quest for beauty, what it is, and its relation to truth, has been my religion. Every seeker longs to meet one who has found; and my longing led me eventually into the presence of one whom I recognized as the very personification of Truth and the very embodiment of Beauty; that Ideal or Perfect Man, whose occurrence on the earth is recorded by history and literature, in whom the existence of an absolute Truth and an absolute Beauty is proved and through whom they proclaim themselves.

If I had been born in another time or place, I would have only sung His praise — analysis and comment would never have occurred to me, they being foreign to art (except when, after becoming a real artist, one by choice becomes a teacher).* But being born when I was and having lived my life in a portion of the world in which all utterance is contaminated by self-interest, the avoidance of comment is impossible. I ask the reader to allow that although some of this comment may seem harsh, it is directed at conditions rather than at persons — it is personal only to the extent that persons are identified with conditions, the world of false values that I attack, and that I myself, my own condition, is the target it has hit before it touches anyone else: "myself" being the world of false values, because it is "myself" who, by

* See Notes.

7

having turned away from the eternal truths, from the "virtue of man" created the false values. But I hope my comment will sometimes be entertaining.

In the years of trying to absorb the truths of Truth and Beauty, I have been as a pygmy wandering among giants, trying to pick up the elements of their speech. And in the writing of this book I have been supported and encouraged only by the smile of the King of the Giants and the faith of a few friends.

What I have written may be of some value to others; but if not, not. That is their affair: mine was in the writing, and in the continuance of that course which "I" once set but which is now in the hands of my Beauty and Truth, Meher Baba.

Foundation

Self (Paramatman) is "One, Indivisible, Infinite and Eternal". This Self is the innermost self of each one of us. It is the sole Creator of the universe and of the world and beings which inhabit it. This creation is created and exists only in imagination in the mind of Self — it has no *real* existence. But Self identifying itself with its imaginary creation deludes itself that it is actor, and experiences the resultant pleasures and pain of action.

In the world of men, according to the shape and colour of the physical form it has assumed, to the degree of energy that activates this form and the quality of mind that informs it, Self identifies itself with a particular race and people and period and culture, as being a man or woman having strength or weakness, beauty or plain-ness, industry or laziness, success or failure. It indulges in psychological subterfuge at all levels in order to augment or diminish its own impressions or its particular identifications and it views all forms and conditions in the light of these particularized impressions.

What is called the everyday life of a man, is Self identified with a particular form—which has no existence except in its own imagination—experiencing through expression (and in experiencing, exhausting) a certain fund of impressions, and acquiring a fresh stock; from which experiencing it retreats or escapes each night in sleep only to be awakened the next morning by these impressions clamouring for expression.

The consciousness of the majority of us may be likened to one, removed to a distant place, closing his eyes and vividly picturing re-association with family or friends, the picturing being so vivid that for the moment he imagines he is actually and really with them. When he opens his eyes again, he opens them on to the scene of his present surroundings—the persons and place of his picturization have vanished. In the same way does Self, closing its eyes to its own boundlessness in which it enjoys absolute power, knowledge and bliss, experience as real the worlds of its own imaginary creation.

To use another figure: the eye can see everything before it but cannot see itself. When a mirror is placed between it and what it has been seeing, it sees only itself — it cannot see any of the things it has been seeing. Similarly, when Self "looks out" on its creation it sees only this creation (which its imagination has created) and it does not see itself. But when it looks at itself in the mirror of Truth it sees

9

itself, and creation disappears. In imagination creation existed; in Reality it has no existence.

Self, in us, remains entranced with its imaginative creation; yet, at the same time, because of its continual frustration through the experience of limitation and because of the ceaselessly changing conditions of its environments it exerts itself to break through the boundaries of limitation and to stabilize conditions so that it will enjoy a somewhat permanent well-being.

However, the permanent solution of the "problem of life" cannot be found in the success of attempts to "push back" the physical limits obstructing knowledge or in controlling those factors that determine the conditions of living, because, even granting success, consciousness will still not be emancipated from the domain of its own imagination — and its resultant frustrations will be merely of a different order. That is granting success, whereas in actual fact, success can never be achieved because the very minds of those attempting a solution along these lines are also only the product of imagination. It can never be anything more than the unreal trying to solve the unreal, or the dreamer trying to understand the riddle of his own dreaming. The only lasting solution can be *only* by Self (which is none other than the real self in each of us) disillusioning itself from its own false imagination and realizing in experience its natural condition of Unlimitedness and Unchangingness.

If this is objected to as being "escapism" or "denial", I reply that since, as shown above, everyone of us each night seeks, with varying success, to escape both from the successes and failures of the day, and since our very programs of progress demand for their carrying out a denial of fundamental liberties both for ourselves and for the peoples these progresses would encircle or crush, the use of the words "escapism" and "denial" becomes absurd. Escape and denial consists in the refusal to correctly ascertain the structure and constitution of the world and Man (and such ascertainment is within the reach of all) and to draft proposed solutions upon the basis of undeniable fact. This is a real denial of intellect and an escape from the conclusion which its relentless use — the unswerving application of the method of science and the unflinching pursuit of art — would force us to accept.

True humanity, and the only possible ground of brotherhood, lies in the recognition that Self is One and is the only Existent Being. In the pursuit of the realization that one *is* that One, lies the only solution to the "problem of life".

Escape is certainly to be longed for and planned and worked towards — escape from the prison of aggressive wanting engendered by our ignorance of truth; denial is certainly to be practised—denial of the false self for the true Self. Self and self cannot live together: either Self is denied for self; or self must be denied for Self. Our superstitions and false freedoms already brand us as escapists and deniers; it becomes us now if we would maintain any semblance of manhood to deny the supremacy of ignorance and escape from the bondage of ourselves.

10

It is, I think, commonly accepted that the slave is the last one to revolt and attempt his own emancipation from slavery. He has to be roused to action and awakened to the fact that he can obtain a vastly better condition by those who, being outside his conditions of misery, are moved by feelings of humanity or compassion and have the intellectual equipment to fight those responsible for and controlling the enslavement.

The supreme Arouser and Awakener is known as the Avatar, the Messenger, the Christ. He is Self completely and perfectly aware of himself as Self. Because of his compassion for men he directly and voluntarily assumes human form for the relief and emancipation of all humanity from its enslavement by greeds and passions and its self-imposed oppressions and misery.

Since Self is One, indivisible and never two and Manyness is an appearance only, it necessarily follows that Avatar, who is that one, indivisible Self, is the actual real self of the apparent many individual selves of us. It also necessarily follows that since Avatar is that Self knowingly by having experienced and overcome the illusion of apparent appearance, and is not an apparent self subject to illusion, his consciousness cannot in any way become entangled in the seeming creation and thereby diminished by his assumption of form since this assuming is the voluntary outcome of his own free will.

The stress and havoc and cry of our times has "brought down" or brought into actuality for us this Avatar.

The prerequisite for His help, this time no less than when He was called Jesus or Krishna, is surrenderance. Modern man, cheated of the fellowship which his "democracy" promised and forced more and more to surrender to authority which betrays and even threatens to exterminate him, becomes alarmed when faced with the idea of further, even total, surrenderance; and because alarmed, assumes a disdain and even contempt for those who have had the courage to make this surrender. We have long forgotten that democracy is based upon surrenderance — surrenderance to one another in gentleness, to the humanity of ourselves in trust, to the ideal of Self in natural enthusiasm — and we have become essentially aggressive. We have become cowards making out we are heroes. We demand proof that, first, Self *is* One, that our brother *is* our brother; second, that an individual man can be the conscious totality of that Self; and third, that he whom others declare to be Him, *is* Him.

The first two proofs may be obtained by (1) an honest intellectual inquiry — as stated in the Katha Upanishad, "Go back from effect to cause until you are compelled to believe"; (2) a thorough examination of suffering and its causes—as recommended by Gotama Buddha; (3) practising renunciation of oneself as one is—as required by Jesus; (4) living the attributes of real humanity (trying to become a real human being) as demonstrated by Mohammed. The third proof rests upon the evidence of His authority and His works — the authority of love and the works of love. This proof must be sought personally in His presence.

We are required, paraphrasing the opening lines of Sankara-charya's Viveka Chudmani, "to surrender ourselves to this One who is the end of all knowledge and its questing, the goal of all love and its suffering — the only Self, the Bliss." But He, although the only one with real authority, unlike the authoritarians, demands nothing of us; we are left free to make the demand of ourselves — we may remain surrendered to our own inadequacy and futile aggressiveness or we may surrender to our own realized Completeness and Unity as manifested in Him; we may retain our hardness of separate identi-fication or willingly dissolve ourselves in our own Being of Love.

"The Ocean becomes drop. The drop-becoming-Ocean has to drown itself in itself to realize that it always was the Ocean."

Out of THAT NOTHING MIND came
Out of Mind came *this* everything
Out of Mind came Energy
Energy holds *this* everything
Out of Mind came *this* Matter
Matter means *this* everything
This everything is also NOTHING
                    coming out of THAT EVERYTHING

This nothing has come out of THAT NOTHING
THAT NOTHING came out of THAT EVERYTHING
This nothing has taken the form of everything
                    which is not EVERYTHING
Out of formless EVERYTHING formless NOTHING has come
Out of formless NOTHING formful nothing has come

We must lose ourselves in order to find ourselves.
     Thus loss is gain.
We must die to self in order to live in God.
     Thus death is life.
We must become completely void in order to become
                         completely possessed.
     Thus complete *emptiness* means absolute FULNESS.
We must become shed of selfhood in order to become
                    absorbed in the infinity of God.
     THUS NOTHING MEANS EVERYTHING.

MEHER BABA

13

Contents

Book I — *Meher Baba*

the occurrence of Reality in illusion

Wings toward the glaciers of Kailas where the first Fathers nourished
The seed of God; and Siva gentled Ganga, and Parvati
Walked by streams of living heart. For Siva was Jesus before him
And Parvati his loveliness in the earth — as was Rama, as was Krishna,
As was Abraham and Zarathustra and Buddha and Mohammed and their
     loveliness —
God's Avatar: as is now BABA. Sing, Baba, your descent this time on earth,
Your Brightness in our night, your comfort in our separation.

For it is my love's desiring, Baba, to compose a book on this theme
Which you set me — and to this task my spirit spreads its wings,
Only to fall stifled and overcome, the song groaning within my breast,
Impossible of utterance. For only a Perfect Master can speak a book,
And saintship is the least qualification to sing of you, although
A profound scholarship is sufficient for the assembling of mere facts:
But I have neither devotion nor learning for the task.

In the past you had Vyasa and Homer and Valmiki and many others
Who were your Name and yourself to leave your Name in impassioned
     prisonment
Of words; and saints innumerable who picked up the threads
Of your Name's loveliness and wove them into bright-patterned verses.
Only if you, Baba, sustain my flight, give knowledge to my intellect,
And unbind the empathy of my heart, can this work be done —
Not miracle, but faith: faith that is grace and grace your miracle.

Ignorant men, men of domestic culture, say that Jesus was the first bringer
Of love. Despicable is their doctrine, having it that before this
God was loveless. And other ignorant men have it that love now is sealed—
That there is no further need of His descent and Example. Love
Does not admit of a first or a last: God is never of more nor less.
All his bright Messengers were nothing but love
And the essence of love, sun-bright and wholly perfect.

Moses was this, for he said, Love God with your whole heart and soul.
Sakyamuni was this, for he showed men the Way of release and bliss.
And the twenty-four Buddhas before him, for they all were Releasers.
Zarathustra was this same Flame, because he told men, When
You behold the sunrise, or, by your hearth-fire, remember the light
In your hearts. Rama was this, because his arrows were a rain of love.
Abraham was this, because he told men to destroy their idols.

And of love was Pallas Athene, because she put courage and wayfaring
Into Telemachus' heart. And of love was Apollo, because his sign
Was the sun, and whatever men love is of the sun, whether of sky or of
    heart,
Whether of creature or of God. And of love and in love was Chaitanya,
For he repeated one word, "Krishna"; and was Sankaracharya this too,
For he said many words explaining that all men were God. And
The rest of them — the eighty-four thousand who were nothing but love.

But if we would name a First, a clear Emblem amidst
The lovely occasions of God, let it be Krishna, whose flute
Is the multitude of men's hearts from the dawn of time till now.—
For if God did not love music, the world would never have come into
    being;
And if men did not love music they would never get to God. It is
Better to reverence all His names, and say "BABA", who is the love now
And the glory and the awakening and the afresh path-setting.

———————————

This time God took birth at 5 a.m. February 25th, 1894. His parents were
Sheheriarji Mundegar Irani and Shirinbai, and he was named Merwan. The
Place Poona. But his legend had begun when Nature and his mother
Were still preparing the vehicle he was to use for his work here.
She had a dream in which a vast sea of people gazed expectantly towards
    her.
In another dream after his birth, a Hindu goddess bearing in her hands
The trappings of worship, beckoned for the child to be given to her.

Experience confirmed the import of both dreams when one day his mother
Found him playing with a snake. At seven years his interest was
Marbles and kite-flying. At nine he was reading Hafiz. He schooled
Till nineteen years, when one evening as he was going home on his bike
An old woman rose up under a neem tree, called him and kissed him
On the forehead between the eyes and initiated him into Bliss. Nine
    months
Later, in one moment, in a flash, she made him know that he was God.

Babajan was one of the five Perfect Masters of this age. She was a true
Faqeer, the earth her bed, a tree and sky her roof, her food
Whatever the earth through the loving householder's hands gave her —
The way of the loveliest and the greatest of east and west:
"Poverty is My glory." Such was Baba's John to his this-time Jesus.
The others of the Five were Sai Baba of Sherdi, Tajuddin Baba of Nagpur,
Upasni Maharaj of Sakori and Narayan Maharaj of Kedgaon.

The office of the Perfect Five is permanent. Before one "dies"
He raises another person to Perfect Mastership to take his place.
They are the sole functioning of God in the earth, the Guidance of
        creation,
The Grace whereby men love, and travel the path to truth.
When in the sweep of time the cry of men reaches to God, they bring down
The "Son" from the heaven of the "Father" to his mission in the world —
Bring him down wrapped in their love and veiled from knowledge of
        himself.

They choose his parents, attend to every detail of his birth;
Throughout his childhood years they watch him tenderly.
Their's is God's motherhood and His-father's protectiveness;
And when it is time for him to go out to work to his job of world-truing
And soul-inspiring, they give him his own knowledge of himself
And hand over to him his own world and its management; and themselves
Retire, leaving the world empty of God save him — God and God-Man.

Babajan gave him the inconceptual experience of his own reality,
And the world and its worlds, gross, subtle and mental, vanished —
And existed not even as illusion: he alone was, the existent and existing.
This is the bliss that alone may be called the bliss, and which
Alone will exist when his work in the world is done
And he returns to his own-father-self again
Leaving another Five to tend this dusty garden of the earth.

The Five brought him down wrapped in the veil of humanity.
Babajan, with a kiss, unwrapped him to Who he was;
Upasni gave him knowledge of what he was to do, brought him down
Through the seven planes dressed again in the triple-garment of the world,
Though loosely — his God-brightness not diminished: a journey
Of unspeakable agony taking seven years. God had again performed
His periodic miracle of down coming and awakening and returning ...

The time was again God's Avatar. "The time was Jesus. The message
Was the same as Moses. Jesus was the soul of Moses and Moses
Was the soul of Jesus. But it was Jesus' turn." The time was
Sakyamuni Buddha; the message was Adi-Buddha's, twenty-four
        previously:
" Does the Blessed One expound a doctrine which is new and original ? "
" If the Blessed One expounded a doctrine which is new and original
He would not be the Blessed One." "Well said, Sariputta ! Well said."

21

The time was Krishna. The time was Rama. The time was Zarathustra.
The time. The time. The world is wrapped in time, and place
Is men's garment. When it was the time for God to demonstrate
The poverty of riches, He was called Solomon who preached life's vanity.
When it was time for men to practise democracy, He was called
      Mohammed
Who lived among men equally in their joys and sorrows. The words
Of God are the time and place; but the message of the words is love.

The time now is Baba who is the Same-One as the First-One, the
      Ancient One.
Only the squint-eyed see two ones. But the last one supersedes
The one before, else it were idle for One to come again —
His first-coming would have been sufficient to the end of time;
And God would not have had the great pleasure of renewal with his lovers
Or of meeting his future devotees. Imagine anyone taking the trouble
Of making a world and only visiting it once!

The last one is the same as the first. But the last one is the seal
Of the message, giving it the imprint of his last-present form.
And if you worship one of his previous forms — if you have
Got into the habit of doing this — whatever blessings
God gives you is only by his grace in his last-now form. Read
"God Speaks".—This present writing is only his light seeping through
Forty-nine degrees of non-illumination and pointing to that Book.

This delightful and frequent recurrence of God's pleasure
In knowing himself, this well-pleasedness-with-himself,
This perfect Vanity of his, is one of the amazements of his lovers
And is the cause of their tears of joy and impossible sighs:
For the lover is in love with the beauty of the beloved,
And the essence of His beauty is his vanity;
And all else but his beauty is vain ...

After God as Maharaj had, with the most finite object, a stone
Begun the down-bringing of that which is most infinite and adorable,
Himself newly awakened, his own new Morning-of-himself for the world;
After he had completed for him the down-coming with its agonies,
And its wonder and glory, and passage-breaking of the atoms of earth
And the rending of the temple veils of heart so that Avatar
Was established in everyone and thing in potentiality of new singing —

22

In the stones and the trees and the animals and in the dust of the earth
And the waters of the sea and in people ready to break
Into lovely song at his Speaking — when all this was arranged
Between himself and himself to his satisfaction and to the amazement
Of all beings illumined and in the hope of all beings still in the dark
Of their turning, Merwan took leave of Upasni and returned to Poona
Where a hut had been built for him on the outskirts of the city.

Now he began to gather his disciples; it was one of these
Who first called him Baba, Meher Baba or Compassionate Father.
Some felt his light in their hearts and came;
Some picked up the hint from Babajan and Maharaj, for these Masters
Were now openly declaring him: "He is now capable
Of moving the world at a sign from his finger." "I have given
The key of my treasure to Merwan — do what ever he tells you."

Some he drew directly to him, using the patience
Of a master lover, flattering their whims, widening gradually
The space in their hearts to receive his love; playing upon
The flute of their hearts till their souls' ears became enamoured
Of his music; drawing ever more closely the net of love about them
And pulling them in from the terrible ocean of conditioned existence
Where they swam with the millions other fishes of us bright-hued or dull.

One, who had been his school-fellow and was unaware
That the universes and the wonders of the six planes lay at his feet
Baba greeted in well-meeting, left the veil across his eyes
And resumed the friendship at its former level,
Indulged mutual inquiries recalling episodes
And incidents and engaged in discussions on philosophy
In which subject, his friend had become adept.

Left the veil and led him on — as a hunter veils the quarry with security;
Then suggested that he himself sweep out each morning the small hospital
He owned. He did; and within six months had swept away his practice
And was free to follow God. So God plays out
The little plays of men. If it's worth a consummation
It's worth a wooing! The sudden sun burns on the west of the ridge
But on an east slope draws up the plants to growth gradually.

Like the chap who had two valuable pots, dirty. One he gave
To one man to clean, the other to another man. One back
The next day, shining, but the temper gone out of the metal;
The other returned after forty days of careful cleaning also
Shining, and useful. It takes time to scour pots or grow tomatoes;
It takes a lot of time to clean out a man's heart and grow love in him
So that as well as being bright with God he can be useful to men.

Love's claiming of another lover also followed an excursive course.
"At this time," this one said, "I used to visit a friend's house
Where we young men discussed everything under the sun.
One night there was a new face. No one paid particular attention
To him, but gradually he seemed to become the focal point
Of the gatherings and it was his say that was granted. 'Merwan
Says this; Merwan says that.' I got sick of hearing his name.

"But incidents occurred which puzzled my intellect
And nagged intelligence for answer — as on a boat excursion
When we went ashore on an island. It was noon
And being a Moslem I went off and found a secluded spot
And offered my prayers. When I got back Merwan was grumbling
That we had all left him, 'One goes off and offers prayers,
Another goes fishing.' None of us had said what he had intended doing.

" I found I was always thinking of him. I told him one day
I was going on a train journey. He said it was a coincidence
He was going on the same train. Soon after we started he said gently,
'Ask anything you like of me — long life, wealth, fame —
And I will see that you get it. But the better thing would be
To make up your mind to do whatever I tell you to do.' My mind was
        made up.
I have followed this Man now for thirty years and obeyed him."

But another as a boy when sick needed only a few visits
To wonder at a kindness greater than his parents'. And when again well
Asked his father's permission to give up his life for him. But his father
Saw no good in this man and forbade it. But in Baba the boy had seen
His true father, so he saluted his father and went to him. Another
(But with his father's blessing) left his home set
In desirable gardens and gave up his life to him.

24

When Baba had gathered to him forty men, he left his hut by the roadside
On the edge of Poona, and accompanied by them walked to Bombay,
And there established his first and ideal ashram, Manzil-e-Meem,
The House of the Master. Here the disciples lived under a strict rule.
Baba was their mother and father: as the one he served their every need;
As the other, he taught them and chastised them of their hindrances
To pure Self — a caring and instructing perfect in method and result.

His transition from one role to the other was as swift
As one turning from the moon to look at the sun
When both are in the sky; and his expression of mood as extreme —
The cool gentleness of the moon, and the fierce burning of the sun.
Gold is the face of the moon to the eyes of children and lovers,
And gold is the sun in the blood of nursling heroes; and the moon-sun Man
Is the gold of God in the hearts of hero-lovers.

So fierce at times was his sun-glory, that disciples of powerful physique
(One a noted wrestler) would tremble before him,
For they knew the power of that slight hand from a body wasted with
        fasting
Which could knock them down with a blow, or pick them up
As though they were rag dolls and crash them to the floor;
While the timid would hide until the sun's storm had passed
And in the sky of their vision smiled once more the smiling moon.

We have been evilly brought up — and there is no evil
Like ignorance or wilful distortion of the truth of God's Avatar —
To the view of Jesus' sacrifice without this view balanced
By an understanding of his glory, his divine terribleness. The Lamb
Has been shown to us — the Lion, Creator and Sustainer and Destroyer
Of universes and lives, suppressed: a pernicious doctrine,
Fosterer of subjection and tyranny; betrayal of truth and love.

We have been brought up on a story, the wholeness of which, is perfect,
But which, in its telling, only half was told — of the Lamb being killed;
The other half, in which the Lion rose with a roar which shook
The whole earth, has been left unsaid. "He suffered the slaughter
Of his Lambness and slept for three days in his cave on the mountainside.
Then joined his Father ruler of wide heaven in judgement on us —
For ours is the sin." An opiate teaching for an indolent people.

The full-eared harvest of the lovely tale of God's Avatars
Has been wasted; and the straw heaped in two heaps for us to feed from.
O betrayal of the majesty of Jesus! "They belittle their Lord
Who make him a mere miracle-worker" and a sacrifice —
Slaughtered lamb for a race of meat-eaters! Feed us, Feed us;
Make our profits bigger, expand our industries. Thank you . . .
Idiots we have been, served by servile doctors.

But our anger at the deception has bred in us violence upon violence,
Grovelling upon grovelling, and divided us in terrible separation.
O Jesus — Bright Morning in succession of Bright Mornings
In the Day of God. Most perfect Morning along with each other
Perfect Morning — Morning for whom the stars called. Morning each time
For whom the universes patiently suffer their tireless turning.
Arrows-stream Morning — Morning-now-BABA.

Brought up on a half doctrine we have been — music
On instruments without completion of lovely speech of song —
The lesser half: for music is in all nature, but speech
Is alone of man: and God's sacrifice in each of his Avatars
Is felt by all things in the earth, even stones and trees,
But His glory is understood by men, and men, by leave of the saints
Can tread the path to it, and by the grace of the Perfect Masters attain it.

We have been told of God's sacrifice for us, but not instructed
Regarding our required sacrifice to Him — surely a doctrine
For shopkeepers who don't like fair trade. We affirm "Unless one die —"
And take it that affirmation is sufficient to bring about our death —
Our beloved Master would never think of helping us along!
It has not been lovingly explained to us that a blow
From the hand of God is a caress from Him of most love.

The Crucifixion of Avatar is continuous. Krishna's disciples
Witnessed it as the Divine Flute-player, struck with the poisoned arrow,
Cried His cry in their hearts to awaken. Jesus' disciples knew it;
And Rama's, when lotus-eyed Sita was torn from Him
And He on the battle field and the muscles of His body like whip-cords
And the sweat pouring from it. And thou, Baba, with your broken body
And the thorns of our heedlessness in your gentle flesh.

26

Bright jewel. Bright jewel. Your greatness is in your humiliation,
Your sun-glory is in your moon-gentleness;
From your suffering is born all singing.
A ray, Beloved, from the jewel of your pain — an arrow-ray
A sudden-rifle ray in this density called heart,
That my soul enwrapt in a shadow-coat of your glory
May sing you, and continue to unfold the story of your love.

Listen to the delightful story of the mercy of God in the form of Tilopa
And how he brought up Naropa from the gate of hell and bestowed on
     him
Eternal Bliss of Truth. Naropa was a bright young man, earnest and
     gifted.
One night he was engaged in a liquidation-ritual for someone
He didn't like the look of when an angel appeared and warned him,
"If you can't absolutely guarantee him a better birth next time
You yourself *could* drop back the rounds even to stone-stage again."

This gave our young dabbler in lives a terrible fright, as no doubt
It would have any usurer or manipulator or other human-trafficker
If they had been so told by an angel or anyone who could shine
Sufficiently brightly; so he asked the angel what he'd better do,
And the angel said, "Luckily I just got here in time — so and so's limbs
Are not yet unstrung, nor his soul shortened of experience.
Go find Tilopa who is the Jesus of this time. He can save you."

So Naropa tramped off inquiring as he went did anyone know the
     whereabouts
Of Tilopa saviour of men. None did. But he would come across a butcher
Skinning a beast who would ask him to lend a hand. And our honours
Student would be palely offended, and a Voice would say, "Too bad
Young fella, that was I, Tilopa who asked you." Or come up with someone
Swigging plonk who would offer him some. But he was choosy who
He drank with, and the Voice would say, "That was I, Tilopa who asked
     you."

It was not long before our young friend developed chronic anxiety.
But eventually he caught up with a real flesh and blood Tilopa
Sitting by a water-hole picking the bones of fishes and snapping his fingers,
Whereat the bones became reclothed with flesh and the fishes plomped
     back
Into the water-hole. Naropa flung himself in the dust and grabbed his feet
And begged him to be reasonable and allow him to go along with him.
And Tilopa, who had all this time only been teasing him, allowed him.

27

Now Naropa's real troubles began. Life with Tilopa was one long
And unfailing embarrassment as exampled when a bride and her escort
Of male relatives passed, and Tilopa said, "I want that girl — get her."
Naropa was left half dead on the road. Tilopa hadn't even waited.
But all roads lead eventually to the Master's grace — and Naropa's
To a camp fire one evening and Tilopa whacking him over the head
With a chappal (shoe) and knocking him up to the seventh plane of God.

Another story dear to devotees is the story of Jelaluddin, glorious
Light of God — so he became; but first, wrote books of the-ol-ogy.
One day he was hard at his next opus (which no doubt would show 'em)
When in walked a Roadsman debonair and dusty who laughed
At all this bookmaking, this darkening of counsel
With words without wisdom, this heaping up of straw for the ass
Of intellect to feed on, instead of being busy with "O God — O God."

He must have been ready for "turning", getting tired of
Trying to get gold out of lead, make fire with green wood,
Grow grapes in waterless sand, irrigate an orchard
With a bit of piddle; trying to fashion
Likeness of God in himself and others without possessing
A breath of silver to inform form — because he took the hint
And started tagging around with his new friend whose name was
        Shams-e-Tabriz.

Now, Tabriz is the name of the city where they lived, and Shams in Persian
Is the name of the sun — which means this man was the glory of that city
And as bright as anyone this side of Mohammed. As Jelaluddin later wrote,
"When the Sun of Tabriz showed His face, the sun of heaven
Hid his face for shame." (See "Mathnawi" — a very Ocean
And a Mirror to be avoided if you would not suffer drowning
Or sight of thy soul's foulness.)

So tender was Sham's heart, that after he was flayed alive
And maggots infested his flesh, when he walked and any dropped off,
He would pick them up and place them back on his person, saying,
"This was created for your food, eat of it." This had come about
Because the king's son had died and the king hated religion and ordered
The priests to restore the boy under pain of religion's abolishment.
But they being only priests were more skilled in words than in magic.

So they begged Shams to be their Moses and Jesus and breathe on the boy
With his life-giving breath and restore order where ruin
Had already begun to unshapen his shapeliness. As the fool
Whom Jesus suffered to accompany him asked Jesus to bring to life
Some bones they came across in the desert; and Jesus exclaimed,
"Lord, is it possible that a man can be so lost that he prefers
Dead bones made living than his own living soul restored to wholeness."

Now, although Shams had the example of how Jesus was rewarded,
He had pity that the people should not be deprived entirely of religion,
So he went to the palace and stood before the dead boy, and cried,
"In the Name of God, arise !" But the boy's spirit did not cast off
Death's veil, because "In the name of" is not the name — as any lover
    knows
That talking about love does not move a woman to take off
Her clothes even on a hot night; only, "I love you" is effective.

Then Shams of his own divine authority commanded, "I bid you rise !"
And the boy's spirit hastened to obey, and returned, and sat up.
Then the priests, those incompetents who but for Shamsuddin would
    have
Perished miserably, cried, "Blasphemy ! He has equalled himself
With God. Flay him ! Flay him !" So the king handed Shams over
To the anger of their shamelessness. Such was the man whom Jelaluddin
Had the supreme fortune to meet and become his disciple.

But ignorance is not replaced by Knowledge until the mind's stream,
Fouled with the bodies and wreck of countless lives, is drained off,
The channel dredged and the sweet waters of eternal Existence let in.
So Shamsuddin, all-loving and regardful of his pupil's future glory,
Disgraced him before the Moslem community by making him carry
Openly through the streets a demijohn of wine.
And threw his precious manuscripts in the well.

But the trials of love are not longer than needful for purgation
Of unlove, as the wheat threshing is not longer than the separation
Of the chaff from the grain, and Jelaluddin's
Came to an end one night after a game of chess. "Lost again,"
He cried. But Shams smiling like destiny wrapped in love said,
"No, this time you've won." And struck him a blow and dispelled
His ignorance forever. Then was the Father again well-pleased ...

"Let us return to the tale. But when did we ever leave the tale?"
That which furthers our argument is not really a digression. The point
We have been explaining is that the true Master has two sides, the gentle
And the strong, the smooth and the rough — just as the world of people
Has two sides to it, the woman, whose mystery is in her gentleness,
And the man, whose strength is in his pride; these two,
The shadows of the shadows of the loveliness and glory of God.

" The Manzil-e-Meem lasted as long as the money lasted.
Then we came over to Arangaon," Baba said. Arangaon,
Village on the Deccan Plateau five miles south of Ahmednagar,
Edge of monsoon belt, dry, only eight to ten inches sometimes. They did
    not
Settle here, but were soon off on the roads again, for a whole year
From place to place as far as Iran, with Baba fasting, not
For his own sake since he is perfect but as part of his work for men.

" For reasons of work I was then doing
I took food and drink at fixed intervals of thirty-six hours
Or more. At times for a week or two at a stretch
I remained on a few sips of tea, milk or soup each day,
Suffering weakness as anyone else who fasts."
Always they would be going to settle, but as soon as the disciples
Began arrangements, he would order the wandering resumed.

Finally they came back to Arangaon and settled on a paddock
Which a disciple had bought outside the village, and on which was
A stone water tank (military purposes '14-'18). Stayed four days.
Came back again for eleven days. A third stay of two days only,
And a fourth of three months. Each time, camp clearing,
Water carting (the tank was empty), building —
First period of gamela yoga (hard yakka) for the disciples.

A windy, desolate slope, everywhere overgrown with thorn bushes
And infested with snakes and scorpions. They cleaned out
The tank for a meeting-room and added a story for a dormitory;
Laid out a garden, built a stone-cavity earth-filled wall
Around the lot. Piped water from a well half-a-mile away.
Built a small room of stones and lime for Baba where he sat
When he did the other sort of work he does while he is here.

30

In January 1925 Baba settled in permanently — as far as "permanently"
Can mean to a man to whom the too-solid earth itself
Is but a moving shadow across the margin of Existence-Bliss.
In July same year he began that SILENCE which he will not break
Till he speaks that Word which will release another Noah-flood
Of destruction of falseness, and of His-Ark (Refuge and Sustaining and
Bliss-transforming place of all that is true and useful to good) upbearing.

That same silence he returned to as was
Before he spoke the word which was his question, "Who
Am I?" and birthed a world of universes and a universe
Of three worlds; spun them upon the axis of his own Name
And groped his way through all the forms to man,
To Perfect Manhood. The same silence, but now
Of Knowledge-Bliss — pregnant equipoise of action.

Now he made a setting for the jewel of Selflessness, built
A scaffolding for the House of Service: he built a hospital and dispensary,
A boys' school and shelters for the mendicant and the migrant poor.
In a model township of three hundred souls, class was abolished and creed
Each one's affair, and they who are called "untouchable" freely mingled.
Each served, and received service. Baba bathed the boys, washed clothes
And cleaned latrines. The disciples had sparse food and he less than they.

He had a table 7′ × 5′ set up by the road and three sides of it enclosed.
In this, at night, he wrote his Book, and continued by day
His other activities. "Between certain hours I freely saw visitors.
Hundreds came to see me believing in my spiritual status,
But most of them only sought my blessings hoping to obtain health
Or advancement or spiritual powers, or a good marriage for their daughter.
Sometimes the stream of visitors continued from morning till evening.

"On one occasion a man wanted to give me everything he had
And begin a new life of renunciation and service. 'Everything'
Turned out to be a wife and seven children. On another occasion a yogi
'Determined to find God at any cost,' sought my instructions. I told him
To wait for Him under a tree. He waited seven days; on the eighth
Preferred his life to God. But there were real seekers, like one
Who kept seclusion and silence even when a cobra came into his cell."

The yogi bit, reminiscent of the chap who came to a Murshid
Wanting God above all else. "Chuck him in the river"
The Master said to his disciples. They did. When he came up
The Master said, "Shove him under." So, two or three times.
Then fished him out. Said the Master, "What didja want most
When you was down there?" "Air," said the aspirant. "Damn fool!"
Said the Master. "If yer'd wanted God I'd 'ave given yer Him."

The Boys' School was unique in this work-ticket-education age,
But as schools were when men were near to God: subjects necessary
For livelihood efficiently taught —" The target is that bird
In yon tree. Describe it." "A bird's head with an eye in its middle, Sir."
"Shoot!" But most and first the pupils were unfolded into men of love —
In the manner of God (Akhlaq-Allah), centred in quietness
And obedient to the seasons: equipped for planes-faring:

Men who as householders lived in abstinence — Ashram-sanyasis —
Loving God and God in men, feeding the stranger before themselves,
Giving innumerable Jesus-cups of water to the thirsty;
Keeping their servants'— if they had 'em — rest-days according
To the sacred calendar; bathing only in cold water and always
Before love approach with joy to their wives, worshipping Guru — God in
      form —
Longing for the fifty years age flight and the begging-bowl and the road.

Meherabad was your establishment in the world, Baba,
Of the lustre of service, the brightness of casteless fellowship,
Your demonstration that creed is encumberance. Then you abandoned
The place, leaving two disciples as caretakers and took the road again.
It was later that some devotees paved with stone the ground
Under the Box in which you wrote the world's next Bible
And built a tile roof over it to preserve it for later devotees.

This time in your travels you included Africa, Europe, America and
      China.
In U.S. they organized a show at the "Bowl" for your Silence-breaking!
You contacted your Agents: for the Americas, a Red Indian
In New Mexico; for Europe, a man in Rome. You spent a night
In one of your beloved Assisian's caves where you held a meeting of
      Masters
And planned the world-course for the next two thousand years.
You went to Avila, where your saints John and Teresa worked for you.

Feeding the poor as you went — the dull-fingered, vacant-eyed poor;
The patient-in-life-poor, the patient-in-God-poor; the carpet-poor,
The ladder-rung-poor of the betrayers, the brother-poor of another's
    troubles;
The brother-poor of the saints and of God. Washing the feet
Of the most-poor, yourself, your children, your pity — yourself
Baba-poor as was Jesus Jesus-poor, as was Mohammed
Mohammed-poor. " Poverty is my glory. Let me be one day ..."

Feeding the poor — the poor of the poorest poor, us, with our
Little satisfactions, our little pleasednesses, our gutter-triumphs
Over matter; our progress-infested poverty, our gadgets-ridden poverty;
Our cinema-poverty, our radio-poverty, our television-poverty
Because we can't look, and see; because we can't listen,
And hear; because we can't feel, and love. Feed us — O God
Feed us, the ladder-rung poor-of-ourselves us

Because of our great insolence-poverty,
Our heart-dead, ear-dead and tongue-dead in lovely speech-poverty,
Our children's no-parent-to-answer-poverty:
Draw a horse, wind-contender, which you have never seen, little one;
Draw a moo-cow of plenty which you have never seen, little one;
Draw a fierce lion which you have never seen, little one:
We have no lovely stories of saints with which to nourish you ...

" Let me be one day full-fed, and next, hungry." Ay !
One day in His Ineffable Beyondness; the next in His Descentness.—
" I am as one who hobbles his horse and goes to sleep for one night
Under a tree, and in the morning rides on again."
Oh, this theme of poverty could be raved to the end of the days of ink —
Yet poverty, belly-poverty and God-poverty, could not even be touched
    upon.
Give us a few rice grains of love, God, with a little honey of your Name.

Yet is poverty a gentle shepherd of us to our pastures of Him —
Else were we all belly-fat poor cropping mirage pasture
By desert lake, gambolling and nay-neighing to our day's end.
If you love us Baba, make us poor — povertize
Our intellects, belly-slim our works and hopes,
Hunger-pinch our dreams; world-reject us of this pinch-belly world
Where gain is ruin, and comfort and honour, loss.

Up to now, Baba, apart from the training of your close disciples,
Your work had been with the children of the world. Tell now,
Author of worlds and singing, of your work for the next ten years
With the children of God who have given up the toys of guns and
        rackets
And have turned their backs on the world-jungle and its Beasts
And have come out into the open spaces of spirit — the wide plains
And the mountain passes of consciousness where their only playfellow is
        God:

Or, have left the harbour of men having brought the war to a successful
Conclusion and set sail for Home over the trackless sea.
Some are detained in that land whose fruits contain forgetfulness.
Some sit in the Giant's cave plotting his blinding and their escape.
Some are being royally feasted by Aeolus master of winds and music.
Some are engaged in mastering the Tantra of Circe. And some
Have arrived at the island of King Alcinous provider of winged ships ...

Eurylochus he left by the hollow ship feasting: but himself went,
For a strong constraint was on him for the trial of the most sacred Tantra
Which had made beasts of his men, but from which he emerged gloriously
Because God sent him a Messenger of right guidance and he listened to
        him
And did that which he was told; but that Messenger of winged feet
And golden wand came not to the others, for it was not their time
And they wouldn't have listened to the words of his sure counsel.

And he went on to the house of the Goddess and called her Name,
And she heard him and opened the shining door and took him in
And gave him a drink into which she put a strong test. But Odysseus,
Godlike with perfumed Presence and remembering His words,
Drew his sword to slay her; but she embraced his knees and praised him,
"Thou hast a pure mind within thee that may not be enchanted. Thou
Must be Odysseus of whom I was warned would come for the rite's
        fulfilment.

"Let us go up into my bed that in love and peace we may trust each
        other."
But Odysseus answered her, "How can you ask me to be gentle with you
When you have turned into swine those that follow and trust me?
Surely there is still guile in your heart that you would unman
And destroy me when you had me naked before you. Swear to me
That you plan not my hurt." And she swore to him by God that she
Would not harm him. And he went up into the beautiful bed of Circe ...

34

Or plainly, have returned from the lesser war of prides and loves
And class and accomplishment, and have marched out again to the
    greater war
Wherein themselves is the enemy and themselves the victory and reward.
Few among men may enter on this holy war where the battle plain
Is lit with the light of a million suns, and the missiles are music
Which unstrings the limbs and perfumes which furl in forgetfulness
The soldier's awareness of time and place and deed: Or

More plainly still, have taken to heart Tukaram's winged words
And have left open the doors of their house for anyone to loot
And have not backslid and put Krishna to the trouble of providing them
With miserable gold, but have remained steadfast and repeated God's
    Name
Day and night, and when the full-eared grain was ready for harvesting
Objected not to the birds being harvesters — as Shamsuddin objected not
But encouraged them: Eat, little ones of God, this is your food;

Nor with Odin objected to eye-price for sight-giving Knowledge; not
Kullervo-despairing on sword-point in forest, nor
Gorgon-affrighted back into stone, nor Lot's wife petrified with doubting.
Odysseus and Aias and Diomedes these men, and Bran battling the waves,
And Achilles glorious on the battlements with the light from his face
Lighting up the plain, and terrible in the forefront of battle — also
Mightily striving with waters aided by white-armed Hera and Fire.

The children of men seek out pleasant sceneries to build their houses;
The children of God dwell in despised places or by shelterless roadsides —
Their abodes and support are a challenge to their Beloved,
And their Beloved accepts the challenge — for what mother or sweetheart
Can bear to see her child neglected, or her lover in want? —
And charges their souls with His fellowship and sustains their bodies
Against rain and cold and protects them from contagion.

The path to God lies through six ascending planes of consciousness.
On each plane fresh glories are unveiled to the traveller
And new hardships await him. On each plane an annihilation
And an abiding, and imagination (fond man)
Of arrival at the Goal — until by the Master's grace he arrives
At the goal which is the goal wherein he is drowned of the world
And himself and abides in himself as God.

35

When the pilgrim arrives on the first plane he is temporarily lost in bliss.
If he overcomes this delusion he advances to the second plane of light.
On the third, body and world are lost and God's power gained
But not used. On the fourth he may use it or not. If not used,
He comes to the fifth plane; if ill-used, he falls; but if for good,
To the sixth straightly comes to constant sight of God and enjoys
And suffers love, until by Love, this last illusion vanishes.

Those who traverse this path with a Perfect Master as their guide
Are called *saliks* or balanced. They are children
Whose hands their father takes on an excursion, showing them those things
Most good for them, and brings them home to sleep-awaking
Of themselves in Reality. To those who by a ray of His grace
Find the path are *masts*. Infinitely more blessed are they than men,
Albeit they are children wandering alone in the sun, amazed.

It was to these that Baba now devoted himself. Up to now,
Apart from his chosen disciples, he had been a stranger among strangers
For although the world is of him and by him, the world is stranger to him
And he is a stranger in the world. (I am as a man who ties up his horse
Under a tree and goes to sleep, and when morning comes rides on again.)
But now he came amongst his own dear children who knew him.
To the world he gives his compassion, but to his lovers he gives his love.

Taking three or four selected disciples with him he now travelled India
(For it is mostly in India in this age that men love God)
From Bombay to Calcutta, from the Himalayas to Ceylon,
Criss-crossing the miles between, seeking his dear ones in bazaars
And jungles and mountain recesses: as Mother, caring for them;
As Friend, encouraging, and enlisting their service in his work;
As Beloved, receiving their love and giving them greater love.

Now, God, as a man, accepts as a frame the limitations of man without
Diminishing his Godhood — in fact, limitation is the glorious jewel
Of his crown. So it was that God did not use his infinite power
To draw them to him, but suffered the roads to them; nor did he
In his omniscience mark them directly, but sent his disciples
Ahead to follow the trails of rumour and intuition and observation,
And bring them to where he was staying.

36

They were not to mention Baba's name, but must of themselves
Persuade the *Mast* to come with them to see their "brother".
Now, just as a man tinkering and tuning cars or ploughing
A paddock does not, at some stranger's invitation, knock off
To go on a little trip, so one absorbed in the business of God
Wouldn't come with them unless the Master had given them a key
To the door of the saint's consciousness.

But these children knew who called them: but though their souls
Were wholly engaged in meeting God, now that he was summoning them
Into his glorious presence they held back from honour's responsibility
And trouble. They who were camp-fires
Held back from joining the bush-fire sweeping the forest;
They who were creeks and rivers were appalled
At the prospect of being brought into the presence of the ocean.

Chatti Baba, when they went for him, complained he was too busy.
Abdul Qadir Jilani greeted them with reverence and murmured,
"Meher Baba — Meher Baba", and promised he would come later.
Gulab said, "He wants to paint me with the colours of divinity
But I don't want that." And when one pressed his feet in reverence
And spoke softly the Name of God, He cried out, "He has caught me!
He wants to send me to the great Homeland, but I don't want to go there."

The Homeland is the Mountaintop Ineffable which lies across a chasm
From the Yellow Castle or the House of Many Mansions. The House
Is reached by three steps — the first three planes. The threshold
Is the fourth plane, exposed to the hurricanes of desire, dark,
Only heroes may cross. Within is safety and light and music and singing.
This is the House of lovely Song which, on its further side,
Opens onto the Mountain where one now sees beloved God.

But even when God as the Master, Love as the Beloved anxious
For his lover's safe crossing, extends his hand over the pitiless gulf,
Fear and reluctance to cross over into the bliss of union still holds
The lover back; for the crossing is fearful, and fearful is loss
Of all that one knows and is: even as in the world
We mostly prefer the safety and pleasure of visioning
To crossing the space between ourselves and vision's consummation.

The new work began in '39 in Ajmer, jewel that Moinuddin Chishti
Set in the dry Aravalli hills 600 years ago — Moinuddin Chishti
Who ate with his ears, music, which in Persian lingo is "food for the soul";
As did Milarepa in the wilderness; as did Ibrahim b. Adham
When he was crossing the desert "And God was giving me my daily bread
Without exertion on my part"; as did Moses and Jesus and Nanak;
As did — with their ears, or by their breath, or something.

To where, namely Ajmer, came in our time Nur Ali Shah Pathan,
A *hafiz* or rememberer, to teach Arabic; but at Chishti's tomb
Became *majzoob* or drowned in God, and God — perfect, yet help-less to
    men.
And also lived on food invisible for some thirty years.
But sometimes his tongue of habit would name some food
Or say "Cha" (Tea) and his love-appointed attendant would bring it
And he would put some in his mouth and some on his head.

Nor did he know he ate or drank; nor was this his sustenance.
Divine Jelaluddin has explained:
The Man of God is filled without meat, and drunken without wine.
The Man of God is made wise by truth, not learned from books.
The Man of God is a vast and shoreless Ocean. The Man of God
Is a treasure in a ruin — whether he be in a desert
Or Himalayan snows or a stinking hovel in Ajmer.

"Three of us," one told us, "were sent to fetch him.
All day we used our utmost persuasion but he would not budge.
We reported our failure to Baba. He told us to try again.
The second morning same result, although we pleaded, and whenever his
    lips
Framed and his tongue said, 'Cha,' we supplied it. On the third morning
Baba drove passed his house. On the fourth told us to go again. We went
And after a while, taking his hand I said 'Come—' And he came with us."

Baba cut away his filth-cemented clothes: he had not bathed
For thirty years, being wholly as Jesus said one should be,
Perfect as the Father is Perfect — and when Baba had bathed him
He dressed him in fresh, white clothes and fed him and sat with him.
And only God knows what they talked about and what lovely expressions
Of love passed between them. Each morning for two weeks Baba rose
    at 3.30
And went through the empty streets and sat with him for an hour.

It was in Bangalore, a thousand miles south, that Baba now went
To find the peerless Chatti Baba and others. He instructed his disciples
Regarding the ways of these men of God — how they should remain apart
At the beginning and observe how the people approached them
And offered their reverence, what was the particular food or fancy
Of each, and in the same manner make their approach and mollify the
    fad
And above all avoid any action which might offend these darlings of God.

The disciples set out from Bangalore for Trichinopoly where they arrived
In pouring rain. They found none here that knew their languages
Until one, who called himself Sardar Saheb, came forward
And spoke in Urdu to them, and offered to guide them in their venture,
For he loved saints and knew where many lived. They set out by car.
The straight road and the surrounding plain was near submerged
In wrinkled sheets of water which finally slowed them to a standstill.

They caught the last train before the floods washed out the track,
And reached Negapatam that night. Next morning
They found Moti Baba, little old man with very bright eyes,
But deferred their mission till sundown; but he was not there
When they came, but presently returned and stripping off his wet clothes
Which were of seven coats and seven trousers, reclined in his underclothes
And smoked several cigarettes and then asked one near for food.

The one asked had one time been a leper and had begged the saint
To heal him, and was told to take dust from the saint's feet
And rub it on the sores; and being healed, had devoted himself
To attendance on the one by whose grace he had become clean.
When Moti Baba had eaten the love-food set before him, the disciples
Ask him to come with them, but he, pointing to his mud-covered feet
Said how tired he was, he had just returned from he who had sent them.

Next morning, slight shiver of palm-fronds in the pale dawn,
They set out to look for Chatti Baba, singer of glorious song,
Whom they easily found because he was much reverenced by the people
And they knew where he was. They found him along the highway
About that time when the sun had gathered strength enough
To greet his countenance; and they paused
A little way off and observed how the people treated him.

Now these people, because they have not got belly-skins stuffed
With all manner of foods, because their bellies do not encroach
On the space God set aside for a man's heart nor extend up to their eyes
Covering them from clear seeing, are accounted by the economists poor;
But they are amongst the richest people on the earth
Because they truly love God in that they honour His saints—the measure—
For the saints are the presence and glory of God in the world.

Each one of these people of song would, as he came up to the saint,
Throw himself on the ground before him, and he would stoop down
And offer them a pinch of dust and they would rub it on their foreheads
Or sprinkle it in their hair and he would laugh gently and say,
"Go brother, go." And they would go lightly. Then the disciples
Approached and reverenced him and he gave them his shining love but
Would not go with them because of much work he had with his children.

So they returned to Negapatam and left for Trichinopoly.
The rain, still falling, had washed out the permanent-way
So they waded through the floods for six miles to high ground
And picked up a bus to Tanjore, where they found Abdul Qadir Jilani
Resting on a butcher's porch in the dark before dawn — the same
Who murmured with great feeling, " Meher Baba —" and would come
      later.
He was a "ghous"-like mast—one who can separate his limbs from his body.

They went on again through the floods following the washed-out line
With their eyes and sometimes with their feet till late evening, and
Picked up a bullock cart to Trichinopoly and parted from Sardar Saheb
And returned to Bangalore by the eleventh day as Baba had set them,
Grieved because empty handed. Then Baba himself went back with them
To Negapatam, contacted Moti Baba and washed his feet and fed him,
And Abdul Qadir Jilani, collected Chatti Baba, and another, Yusef.

Chatti Baba was a moon-saint incomparably glorious, a wondrous singer
Who gladdened hearts as does a full moon on a summer night
Coming over a hill gladden friends gathered on a veranda
And below them sweeps away a well-cultivated orange grove.
He became perhaps Baba's best worker, although he would gently
      complain
Of the labours put on him. "Ah — He will be back soon," he would say
When Baba was away on a trip." This will mean more trouble for me."

40

Karim Baba was a sun-man of a saint and Chargeman of Calcutta.
Baba first contacted him on a pavement where he had sat in filth
And sun and rain for six years, surrounded by assorted debris,
His throat entwined with tangled skein of fine wire, and bangles
And anklets of rag on his arms and ankles. Such was the glory
That shone from his face and eyes, that world-encrusted men
Were moved to repentance and love by sight of him — glory unbelievable.

Unknown to the few rich (whose special activity in Calcutta as in
New York or Sydney or any other erect and spread mass of concrete
Is cultivation of ignorance of values) he was held in great reverence
And esteem by the poor and middle classes. Whether they knew or not
He held their welfare continuously in his heart,
Something of the dignity and authority of his Office was apparent to them.
Baba contacted him four or five times, fed him and gave him cigarettes.

A few weeks later, a disciple was sent to bring Karim Baba to Ranchi
Two hundred miles north west where Baba had established an Ashram.
At the disciple's suggestion that he come away with him,
The saint gave a short laugh and returned back into himself.
His soul came forward for the moment of his laugh and returned
To its contemplation of God. It came down to the plains in one moment
And returned to its circling of Manasarowar. The disciple retired,

Bought new clothes, posted a cab handy and again approached him
And asked him to stand up and allow him to replace his old clothes
With new ones. To his astonishment the saint stood up, and one by one,
Working carefully and quickly, he stripped off his rags and re-dressed him.
By now a small crowd had gathered, amazed to see their beloved saint
Being undressed and re-dressed by a stranger; more amazed still
When he began to follow this stranger to a waiting cab.

The disciple prayed that their docile amazement might not turn
To belligerent interference at his saint taking away. Next, was to intrude
Into this Sun-emblazoned consciousness the idea and the approval
Of getting its body into the cab. The body sat down on the running-board;
The soul continued its circling flight of Self-contemplation
In the Mirror-lake. The disciple waited Eternity's whim. Gradually
The great bulk hauled itself into the cab and sat on the floor.

Springing in he ordered the driver to drive fast to the station
Where he got Karim Baba into a small third class apartment. Up to now
The great mast had not uttered a word, but when the train-leaving was
    due
He said tersely, " The ticket is taken and the train is leaving." Which
Meant, " I am going to that One who will set me on the last stage
Of my journey to the Goal." And so was fulfilled a saying of Baba
That one day he would have two sixth plane saints living with him.

And others of these lovely moon-children and sun-children of God,
Gods and goddess among men — breastplated and shielded
With silence and withdrawal in clear purpose, who flinched not
From the spear of calamity as it hurtled towards them,
But like Automedon gazed steadily at it keeping it in their sight
And skilfully avoiding it and answering with keen blows —
For whom Baba suffered endless travail :

There was Mohammed, singer with voice of sweet thunder which
    melted hearts
When he sang of Baba and his rescue of souls from the terrible ocean.
And Phulwala who used to weave garlands of flowers and adorn himself,
And who Baba said,"With one slap could knock you up onto the
    sixth plane.
And Pullukollah Baba,"King of all Masts," aged 120 years, whose
    reputation
Was very great because he crossed rivers unaided. And Shahabuddin Baba
Who had not suffered injury when a farmer drove a bullock cart over him.

And Pir Fazel Shah, adept pilgrim, also aged—117 believed, but hale,
Who greeted Baba and his men with great reverence, offering the Master
A special seat and saying: "No one before you came has so pierced my heart
With divine love. No one knows your greatness — if I were to die tonight
I would take another body immediately to be near you." And Moti Baba,
Other than he before mentioned, also adept pilgrim revered by harlots.
And Lakhan Shah wrapped in his divine dream.

And Nawab Ali Shah, who said to a disciple,"There is a place I would go
But the road is closed. But I will ask permission of the Silent One
And if He gives it I will go. And because he knew the disciple came
    from Baba
Gave him presents. And Qadir Sahib, sometimes master, sometimes
    drowned.
And Nasiban Mastani, mastani gitana, by a bridge, old and adept pilgrim.
And Mastani Mai with eyes of a vina, who looked adoringly at Baba

And said: "Allah." And Maulavi Saheb Mastan who was Chargeman
    of Madras.

And Waliji who was ordered to let loose Godavari's flood at Nasik,
And did so. And Qadir Main who also wields God's powers, and loves tea—
Two bucketsful a session. And Maulana Shamsuddin Ulema who
    exclaimed:
"In the darkness of night I see the light of God." And Gadge Maharaj
Who brought the living Vithoba to Pandharpur
And assembled 70,000 people by the river in the moonlight
And they spent the night singing the praises of the living God.

These are some of the names of the lovely ones of God. But lovelier
Even than they are the disciples who have given themselves utterly
To him and journey with him his journeys of work and love. They are
The hands and feet and speech of the Sun and Moon and Beyond of him.
For ten years of sun days and moon months they worked in this work
Of the Divine Sun and Moon and Beyond of Baba,
But it was by his grace that they succeeded in their work.

Sun day and moon month, time, our master
And the Master's slave had now crept in decrepitude
At his blessed feet honouring him for twenty-eight years
Since the establishment of his perfection
And as the Avatar of God had begun to draw to him his disciples,
Calling on them in their hearts, where he eternally dwells,
To awaken, for now was the time again for service.

Moon night and sun day, sleep time and waking, seclusion
Of unconsciousness and coming forth again to loves and hopes.
But the saints reverse this — day is separation and night the time
Of love. The tears of the day are the pearls of men's dreams,
The sighs of the night is the saints' road to God.
And God too has a night and a day — Night of Beyond the Beyond,
And Day of Creation and Sustaining and Destroying what he creates.

On Kailas Siva endlessly enjoys his Existence-Knowledge-Bliss,
At Chidambaram he dances the world into being and gloriously sustains it
And in the Burning Grounds fired by Agni-Hephaestus he destroys it.
The act of creation presumes the preservation of what is created
(Handle thy fragile pot carefully, O potter, and do not spill ink
On your precious poem, poet); the act of preserving assumes destruction.—
God alone knows what I am trying to say: read "God Speaks" on't.

43

God alone knows what any of us are trying to say. His Dance
Has brought confusion upon us — we are intoxicated by the movement
    of it.
Would that we were drunk by His beauty — then would our hearts
Be Chidambaram and the Burning-ground of our desires. Siva-Baba,
Siva-Baba, we have caught a ray from your eyes' light — send fire
To burn out the dead stump of our life's tree. If we are not willing
To be consumed by your love, how can we lay down our lives for you.

We are trapped in a nine-gated house surrounded by bush fires.
Across the valley on the shore of the lake is the City of Spirit crowned
By my Father's mansion. Towering in grandeur beyond this is Kailas itself
Where my Ineffable Lord Baba has his home.—Yet, yet, he wandereth
The city streets, peering in every doorway, looking for me. Nay, fool, look!
He subdueth the fires on the hillside around my wretched shack,
With the water of his tears he quenches a pathway for my feet.

Most copious are his tears — the tears of each one who weeps;
Ganga herself falling from heaven and coursing down his cheeks
And filling the five oceans. A Man of sorrows. It is his sigh
That fills the reed-flute of each heart, causing the sweet music of lips
And eyes and children's dancing. Krishna-Jesus-Baba —
Where your feet have trod on this earth and the planes *through* heaven
Plant thou my feet and bring me home—but not before your work is done.

Moon night and sun day ... and a Night and a Day has God as Avatar —
Night of Light and Bliss in Withdrawal, Day of Descent in which
Nights and days alternate in seclusion and activity.
Baba's first seclusion was for nine months after Babajan had unveiled him.
The world was not; only He was — as in His Beyond Beyond.
But in that he had slept; but now he was Awake. He was awake,
But he worked not, because there was no-where in which to work.

After Maharaj had brought him down, and told him, "You are the
    Avatar,"
He secluded himself again — this time for work of calling his disciples,
Renewing their loves for him, fitting them for the field of the world.
For the next twenty-eight years he alternated work in seclusion
And work in action — seclusion at Meherabad, Meherazad, Angiras Hill
(From which he emerged drawn and haggard and told a disciple
That three-quarters of the world would be destroyed) and many other
    places.

Baba now entered his Great Seclusion of forty days — Curtain between
Two Acts of Old Life and New Life: curtain of author-actor
Writing into the original sketch-plan the detailed parts of the next act.
The forty days divided into: nine days, during which twenty-one poor
And seven men were brought to him; nine days during which
The *work to be done* was done, fasting all the time —"No one knows
Except myself and God what I went through during those nine days";

Six days of partial relaxation and some solid food taken;
Shift of residence in closed car to Poona for nine days and work
With masts, his men scouring the roads and bringing them to him;
And back at Meherazad for final seven days. The Old Life Act finished
And established in potentiality of being in the hearts of the Audience,
The Supreme Actor, God Himself, Lord Baba stepped lightly and
      radiantly
On to the stage for the next act of Utter Helplessness and Hopelessness.

The Great Seclusion was from 22nd June to 31st July '49. On August 15th
Baba called the disciples together and told them of the New Life
He was beginning on October 16th, a life of homeless helplessness
On the roads, and invited whomso would follow him, warning them
To consider it carefully — there would be no return, and himself
Helpless to help them. For now he who had been greatest would become
      least,
He who had been the highest of the high would be the lowest of all.

Those who went with him were to consider themselves already as the dead
Who have no further connection with the living and ask no more questions
And need no provisions for their journey. They must disburden themselves
Of all fads and religious beliefs, and have no expectations whatsoever
Of reward; be willing to die causeless and without reason, as a noble tree
In the forest lives without connection or question and is already dead
Without reason of its own, being marked out by a pitiless axeman.

Then Baba had four of the disciples read from the four bibles:
Avesta, Gita, New Testament and Koran.
And as each reading was finished he took the scripture
In his hands and laid it on a table and told one to pray thus:
"May God help Baba to definitely make this step, which he is taking
To give up everything and go away, irrevocable, so that from October 16th
When he enters the New Life there will be no turning back."

And some were amazed that he prayed to God, for never before
Had he done this, but had always said he was the Same as God —
Perfect, as are all Perfect Masters perfect. And each believed this
Both from his presence and from his acts with others, and their faith
Was not shaken — even those who had been with him since
He had become perfect and established as Avatar by the Perfect Five —
But none thought to say, nor dared if he had thought of it, say, Amen.

Nor would the hardships of the roads of the Mast-trips, the footslogging
And bullock-cart sufferance of endless days and miles, be their hardships,
But the labour, the solid labour of controlling their every feeling
And emotion; not not-feeling, but controlling feeling — catching
It in its bud before it burst into expression: Sadhana of
Mahasadhakas, yoga of mahayogis — Maharjunas of Kurukshetra
Of victory of no-reward, no hope — for love, for dear love.

Yet would he still require of them obedience. " I will live among you
As your brother. I may even fail at your feet or ask you to spit on me.
That is why it will be very hard for you," he told them.
Then he disbanded his ashrams and with what money came to him
Provided for families dependant on him. And when
The glorious morning of their going dawned, they set forth
Gloriously. And they sang a new song — The Song of the New Life.

Vanvas, sanyas, satyanas — exile, renunciation, ruin: " This is the
End of my beginning and the beginning of my end." The pilgrim road
Led on to the conquest of that which is but was not; is, but never was
Anything at all; led on to the destruction of mind, mother of illusion
And delusion of hopes and fears and attachments and separations,
And thirst; spinner of coins of gain and loss; maker of art and bad art.
But God has his own thirst which leads him in the devotee to Himself.

The Perfect Masters enact their roles; Avatar *becomes* the part he plays
For our unveiling: just as in a play well put together for our enlighten-
    ment,
A real play concerning some episode in the life of an Avatar,
An actor is a carpenter and is making a table and acts his part perfectly,
Or another actor for the duration of the play becomes, and does not
Know himself as other than, a carpenter. So Baba became helpless
And prayed to God to help him; and with God's help annihilated his
    mind.

46

And when mind was gone, his Old-Life of Knowledge, Strength and
    Greatness
Abided; but he kept also (by his own act of keeping) the ignorance,
Weakness and humility of the New Life: then was he Himself and us
At the same time. And so there arose in him Life, free and obligationless:
The life of Master and Servant; of knowledge that we are all eternally
    One,
Indivisible and Infinite in essence, but separate through ignorance;
Life of strength in Knowledge and weakness in binding desires.

And this led to the tripartite life of *complicated-free life* in which
Bindings dominated freedom; *full-free life* in which freedom dominated
Bindings; *fiery-free life* wherein both freedom and bindings were
    consumed
In the fire of Divine Love. Now was there a complete blending
Of God-state and Man-state in which the one lived not in opposition
To the other, neither did one encroach upon the province of the other.
And the Divine Truth of his realization he shared with those who sought it.

" Ho ! " says my fool, "if bindings dominated freedom, how could it be
A 'free life'? If freedom dominated bindings, bindings still trailing,
Freedom would not be free." " Listen, sweet fool, God is not false.
He may allow bindings to bind Him, but He is not bound; He may exert
Freedom over binding, but that is not His Freedom. He wears loosely
Both freedom and binding. His bondage in us is our deliverance (in Him),
And our binding in Him our freedom from ourselves."

Now he could again say that he was the Ancient One, the Highest of the
    High.
And in Dehra Dun in '53, on the anniversary of his birth as Zarathustra
He said: " Consciously or unconsciously, directly or indirectly
Every person and every creature strives to assert individuality.
But when at last a man experiences himself as being Infinite,
Eternal and Indivisible, he is conscious of his individuality as God.
To worship such a Man is to worship God.

" When God manifests himself as a man directly, he is known as Avatar.
He is the salvation of all men and the help of all creatures.
Age after age Infinite God wills through his Infinite Mercy his presence
Among mankind by stooping down to human level in human form,
But his glory being covered, he is looked upon as being merely a man.
But when his time of divine assertion comes he is worshipped by some
Who accept him, glorified by a few who know him, but the rest condemn
    him.

"Thus it is that God as man, proclaiming himself as the Salvation of men,
Suffers himself to be persecuted and tortured, to be humiliated and
Condemned by men for whose sake his infinite love has made him stoop
To man state in order that men, by the very act of condemning him,
Assert his existence in his Infinite, Eternal state. The Avatar
Is always One and the Same because it is the One Same God who manifests
In different forms and places to free men from the bondage of delusion.

"In the world there are saints; and many who pass as saints.
The saints are not ordinary men, neither are they on the level of God;
But God gives them of his powers and they can and do do miracles for men,
Satisfying the passing needs of those who approach them sincerely.
But I am not a saint and to seek benefits from me is to court
Utter disappointment. Either I am an ordinary man or I am
The Highest of the High. I am nothing in between.

"If I am an ordinary man I cannot do miracles and it is useless
To ask me to do them; if I am not an ordinary man, and I have assured you
I am not a saint, I must be the Highest of the High, and as such
It is folly to ask me to alter that which I have appointed. If I am the
Highest of the High my will is law, my wish governs the law and my love
Sustains the universe. Rather than ask me to relieve your sufferings
You should lay down your very life at my feet, accepting my guidance.

"But they cannot obligate me who surrender with selfish motive that
Which perforce they must surrender one day, life and possession,
Bargaining these for the treasure of eternal bliss. If I am the Highest
Of the High my role demands that I strip you of all
Your possessions and wants, consume all your desires,
Making you desireless rather than satisfying them;
Take from you the burden of attachment and ignorance.

"I am not for those who stand in rapt admiration before me.
I am not for those who ridicule me and point at me with contempt.
I am not for the crowds who flock around gazing at me.
I am for the few, who scattered amongst the crowd, silently surrender
Their all, body, mind and possessions to Me. I am still more for those
Who after surrendering their all never think of their surrender.
They are already Mine who renounce even the very thought of
      renunciation.

48

"Far more blessed is the atheist who confidently and honourably
        discharges
His worldly duties than the man who professes belief in God yet shirks
The responsibilities appointed him by divine law and runs after saints
Seeking relief from those very sufferings which would ultimately pronounce
His eternal liberation. To have one eye glued on the comforts and the
Pleasures of the world, and with the other expect to experience
A spark of eternal Bliss, is impossible, and the height of hypocrisy.

"You cannot understand now all that I want you to know. It is for me
To awaken you from time to time throughout the ages — sowing in your
Limited minds the seed which must in due course germinate, flourish
And bear the fruit of Knowledge which is inherently yours.
But your own way, though more painful is also your progress to me —
For all progress is mine. If you would be saved that pain, AWAKE now.
Be honest with yourself and God: you cannot escape his knowledge.

"Seek me not as the Highest of the High to take away your troubles,
But find me in order to surrender yourself with your whole heart to me.
Let my happiness be your cheer and my comforts your rest. Beg me not
To save your life but to permit you to lay down your life at my feet.
Never expect me to cure your bodily afflictions, but beseech me to cure
Your ignorance. Never stretch out your hands to receive from me,
But hold them high in my praise.

"If I am the Highest of the High, a wish of my Universal Will can give
In an instant God-realization to one and all; but blessed is knowledge
Gained through the experience of ignorance, in accordance with Divine
        Law:
Knowledge, which is possible through perfect Guidance and surrenderance
To the Highest of the High." Thus Baba fulfilled the sayings of the
        Prophets
"My glory is like the mountaintops." "Before Abraham was I am."
And encouraged us also to become perfect as is God.

Baba-Sahavas, the company of God — but who but God can keep
God company? Elijah walked with God, which means he was one with
        Him;
Radha knew His embrace because she was His own loveliness;
And the saints talk with Him, are Him, inasmuch
As Junaid pointed out to the insolent disciple, they exercise
The powers of God in the earth. But these were not at Meherabad Nov. '55
When for each week of the month 250 men enjoyed Baba's company.

There were, first of all, the disciples: heaven sprung, purely birthed
In again-birth of service which will quit them of service;
Mature men who breakfast on couplets of Hafiz and have wine
Served with every meal; mature men drunken irreproachably;
Precise in action, inwit and outwit as bearings
And piston or propeller-shaft in His act of acting; their lives,
Pouring as rivers into His ocean — heaven sprung, God-returning.

Second, there were the thousand guests of God
Divided into four convenient language-groups of one week each:
The Hindi-speaking ones from Bihar and Uttar Pradesh and Delhi
And as far north as Rikhikesh; the men from Andhra who speak Telegu;
The men from Bombay speaking Gujerati; and the men descended
From Sivaji's men speaking Marathi — comprising all classes
And creeds and temperaments which were laid aside and forgotten;

Or poured together into a heart-lake of His reflection.
They were clustered leaves on His bough, rustling in His breeze;
Or bees pouring after their Queen on her swarming-flight leading them
To a new home; or skipping lambs before His shepherding to the pastures
And clear streams of Him; children before His All-father-mother
Bounty and security. But the disciples were as so many stars to His moon,
Moons to His eternal sun — signposts to the Reality of Him.

And the hundreds of villagers and farmers who rumbled and tinkled by
In bullock-carts, or padded along silently on bare feet that scarcely
Disturbed the dust; and their grave-eyed and laughing children
Who greeted one in the Name of God. And the boy across the paddocks
Drawing water with bullocks, ordering their going and halting
And the flow of lovely water from the cool well-depth
With a musical call that was also a prayer to God in the burning sunlight.

Beside these there was one,
John Kerry, an Irish-English-Australian, in his forty-ninth year —
Threshold, according to Hindu classical and Sufi reckoning, of old age —
There for the whole month. Four times as long on account
Of concrete roads which walked in his sleep and deadened
The feet of his spirit for dance, and machines which whirred
In his dreams, making the hands of his soul inept at grasping the Real.

50

The Flash of God is instant: His lightnings are sudden.
But the hammers of the sun are slow in shaping a man in the likeness
Of a man; slower still in shaping him in the likeness of God.
Seven years and seven years for a bride of loveliness; seven years
And three times seven years for John to meet the Lord of his search:
Twenty-eight years of sun-beat and rain-beat — and one month
Of the Sun-fingers of Baba wiping away some of the stains of the dream.

For Baba was Sun of no sun-beat during the days of this month —
Sun of sun-love, gentle and radiant, as in spring
And the hearts of all men and creatures open in wonder at his shining
And at the earth dressed in her green dress embroidered with white
And gold flowers; and men's hearts are stirred with high adventure.
Days of wonder singing at His presence; and laughter
And sudden silence and weeping for Him — Beloved, Master and Friend.

Heart music — soul in clear singing of song-beginning
As in the dawn of time when the stars sang; song of instruments
And voices trained in love-singing, in which God was praised
And love's states described, and Baba's life-story set forth —
Love singing of love and listened to by love.
The Song of His Silence spoken by his faithful interpreter
As discourses, reminiscences, story-telling and encouragements.

Explained to them love and the ways of love. Took them for walks
Round Meherabad and Meherazad showing them particular spots
Of seclusion and where he had worked with his beloved *masts*; through
Arangaon with the village band leading the way, where people
Worshipped him. Explained love and love's ways to them. Washed the feet
Of a thousand poor, bowing his head to their feet, being the poorest,
And gave each money. Explained love's ways, being himself love.

Explained the way of love: From "beginning" to "end"
There is nothing but God; from "eternity" to "eternity" we are all one:
An eternal, indivisible ocean of oneness. But we do not know this,
Being drops of "I am myself" in the spray of a wave caused by his Whim
For knowledge of Himself. But when our precious human-consciousness,
Focused now falsely on our own bubble of a body, realizes
Who we are, we will know that we, each one of us, is the whole ocean.

In a room one is conscious of its dimensions and of the objects
And other people in it. If one goes outside, consciousness can take in
The surrounding countryside and sky. If one climbs a hill,
A vast panorama can come within the range of consciousness which,
Remains the same consciousness (as the person is still the same person),
But its scope and nature has changed: so, when our consciousness bursts
Its bubble-body identification it becomes conscious of itself as ocean.

We breathe. And the moment we stop breathing, we are said to be dead.
Our life hangs on the thread of our breath, and yet at every moment
We forget it. Yet it goes on, and all night when we sleep, stitching
And holding the parts and functions of the body intact. Only when
"Out of breath" or ill do we remember it; and only when we are drowning
Or suffocating do we unmistakably know that no breath
Means no life, that breath and life are one and the same thing.

We live, yet scarcely conscious that our life is breath.
And infinitely more precious than breath, is love for God. By breath
We remain alive in what is called life, but love for God is the means
By which we realize that our very being is God — our breath and our life
Are nothing but a manifestation in illusion of our eternal Existence.
Not until we are being deprived of breath do we value life; not until
We are being strangled by love do we know we cannot live without God.

Our own infinitude leaves no room for anything to exist outside of us.
This earth and the innumerable universes are but empty bubbles within
The divine ocean of our being, dependant upon our consciousness.
We are filled with wonder at the earth, sky, light, sound,
But they are not there when we sleep soundly. From our waking
We pass through dream to sleep, and from sleep through dreams to waking.
In sound sleep nothing of our wonder nor fears nor hopes were there.

In sound sleep we pass into our original divine Unity, but do not know it:
We wake, and are conscious only of the illusion of our own creation,
The shadow of the oneness of our real existence. To remain awake in sleep
Is to realize ourselves as God and to experience infinite power,
Immeasurable knowledge and unfathomable bliss. By us it is impossible
To obtain this experience; by having the courage to become
Annihilate of ourselves, by the living Master's grace, we attain it.

We are caught within the bindings of the tangled skein of wants.
Whether we want food or want God, want God with all comforts
Or all comforts without God, "I" is there, wanting.
Before the beginning of all beginnings there was no "I"—
Only God was; unconscious of Himself. Then arose the Whim, "Who
    am I?"
Thus the most original want came into being, and that want let loose
On the ocean of His Being a storm of drops. Each drop

Although of the indivisible ocean, was now a separate "I" and forgot
Its want of Self-knowledge and only remembered "I want". Through
The mineral, vegetable and animal kingdoms the wants multiplied,
And the "I" of the drops magnified, until, after countless cycles of time
The original want "I want to know myself" is remembered by us.
This want can only be satisfied by our "I" diminishing
And ultimately disappearing into our infinite Self.

But now, as soon as the path to Self-knowledge has begun,
The "I" runs the risk of being magnified all the more:
"I am advancing!" "I am enlightened!" it says. Therefore one must
Be ever watchful until the "I" and all its bindings actually
Begin to be burned in the fire of divine love, and ultimately
By the grace of the Master the bindings are all destroyed, and the "I"
Answers, once and for all, its question, "Who am I?" with "I am God."

I have explained to you why and how you are God.
But remember that so long as you do not *become* this truth
You will be posing and pretending if you say you are God.
Posing and pretending is the only sin God never forgives.
If you know yourself to be an ordinary man do not pretend to be a saint
And become a satan. If you know you are a scoundrel, you need not think
You are not worthy to love and be loved by God, the Ocean of Forgiveness.

Although from the point of view of drop-as-ocean there is no past
And future, only the ever-present, from the drop-as-drop viewpoint
It requires millions and millions of years to know your own eternity.
You *understand* all this; but when you arrive at *conviction*, if a dog bit you
You would not for a moment forget that the dog and you are one.
This condition of consciousness would be the beginning of knowledge,
The end of which, is the divine authority to assert, "I am God."

It is no joke to love God. He is so infinitely beautiful,
So infinitely precious and so infinitely Infinite,
That even if you had an infinite number of lives and cut
Each life into an infinite number of pieces
By way of an offering to Him of your love
It would not necessarily be enough for you to become one
With this Beloved who is the sum and beyond of all beloveds.

Age after age I come down to give you my love and to receive your love.
Love me. But never let your love escape in words through your lips
To others. To speak of your love is a boasting and an insult to love.
Even a saint can fall through such expressions of egotism.
Love is a flame, and to speak of love is to choke that flame with smoke.
Real love is a clear flame which burns up everything, leaving
Only God. Love me; and when you go from here, take me with you.

Thus Baba explained to them through his love, through the words
Of his faithful interpreter, the ways and the way of love: Love,
Ever lovely and glorious and bright, the One-Being, God, their own Self
Who appears as many but in reality is One; and encouraged them to
      awake
From their sleep in dreams and their sleep in God and their dreaming
In wakefulness and know themselves as God. And their doubts were
      dispersed
As mist before the sun, and they were lifted up to gaze at him in amaze-
      ment.

Thus ... God's descent as a Man; and men near to Him:
The disciples; and the planes men, some
Toiling the terrible smiling passes, some nearly finished their journey,
And one by Grace his journey done; and the many poor
Who are always on the earth; and the thousand and one guests
Who stayed with God; and the villagers who live by His Name:
God, His glory and His gentleness and His brotherhood with men.

The One-Being Who is beyond comprehension of intellect and heart,
But Who is infinitely and immediately knowable in His-Avatar —
BABA: the Same as was called Zarathustra gleaming bright
And pure Intelligence, Krishna glorious Player of heart-music,
Rama of Love's bow and streaming arrows, Buddha of immaculate
      Compassion,
Isa perfect and divine Swordsman, Mohammed perfect Man living
With men, Example and Demonstrator of democracy: the Same, the Same.

54

The One towards Whom Odysseus the now twice-born set up sail in his
    ship
Well-stocked by lovely-haired Circe after she had lovingly tested him
And brought him part-ways on his way to glory. The One, indeed,
For Whom the whole Achaian host strove in fearful labour
To bring back pure and shining moon-Helen and so purely win His grace;
For Whom they made burnt sacrifice of their own desires and poured
Out the wine of their blood in offerings.

The One, indeed, for Whom all ships ever set out over dark seas
And trackless ocean — it is His Shoreless Ocean of Truth they seek;
For Whom all camps and settlement are made and settled and struck
And the march resumed; for Whom all songs are poured, both in praise
Of His last Brightness and in certainty of His next love-bringing —
As are the singers sacrificed of themselves for Him, like crystal glasses
At a banquet, their stems snapped after the royal toasting.

The One for Whom the reckless-of-life ones, the *masts* and *saliks*
Throw away their lives: sunbeat and thirst and mirage sharpness,
Moon-glint and craziness and enwraptment and the hollow night
And the dark night of CALLING; and the calling ceased,
And the blood turned to milk, and tears, tears, tears:
The Path treaders, and the Goal arrivers in you, BABA, and their
Majzoobiyat — drowned, drowned, utterly drowned in your love.

Book II — *The Love Song of John Kerry*

illusion singing to Reality

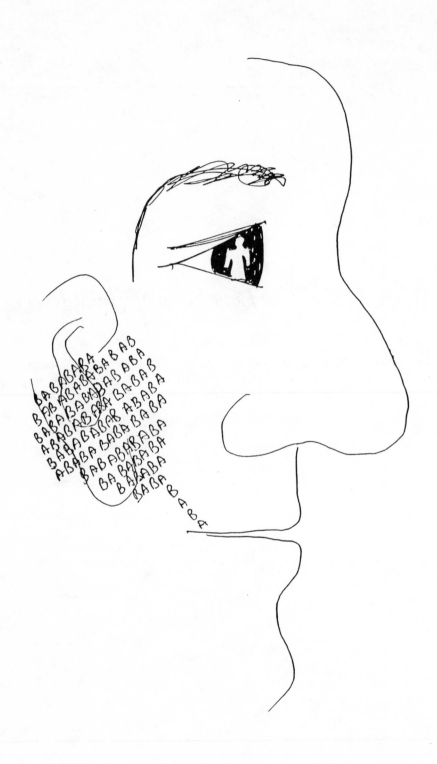

Back in Australia, the most East of the West,
John Kerry continued the exile he had begun so and so
many millions of lives ago through his own act of waking up
and wanting to know exactly who he was —
a musical question which turned out to be
a fugal proposition of infinite possible development.

Sunbeat and rainbeat, veil upon veil — day-veil of brightness,
night-veil of dark; face-veils and form-veils gossamer spun,
crowded close and thickly; sail-veils and flag-veil hoisted
over veil of sea — veil-voyage and returning; rain-veil of weeping
and a place he hoped where none knew of ships and journeying
and the far-shadowing spear of His glance — Baba thou Beloved.

Nursing his wound never healing, but widening
because the spearhead remained in it — widening and love-festering,
sloughing off veil-flesh; widening cleanly and the spearhead of bliss
entering more deeply into the flesh-veils ever more hungrily and healingly,
as the sun into the earth when the farmer sets his plough
more deeply into the sour subsoil where no sun has been before:

Each day of day-drag or day-flight curtained
within the three curtains of sleep-veil and dream-veil and awake-veil —
sleep the forgetter and dream the distortioner and wakefulness
the cruel concretizer who sets the dreams in solid forms, the painter
whose brushstrokes are the bones, and whose colour
is the teeming flesh squeezed out of tubes of nerves:

Nursing the wound nursing the wound, gazing with admiration
on the face of the lovely Spearman, he was saying to himself:
Small wonder and great wonder things are as they are
and this business of Everything and Nothing. This business
of being nothing and somebody, nobody feeling he is something.—
Something, something in your hand, Baba, or else nothing before your
        feet.

Patience, patience fool, he was telling himself. Yap-yap
of nothing about something which turns out to be nothing —
yap-nowt of piddle-pool-puddling, instead of sitting quiet
by the crystal stream gold-flecked of His love. Two advantage when you
sit still: you don't feel the kick in the bones so much — and you give
him a chance to do something — Baba thou beloved — you Baba:

Stop wanting, when you are lying down, to raise yourself onto your knees,
and stop wanting to lie down and cover your head with a blanket
when you are standing up; stop wanting a job, a job with dry land
and with lovely rivers. Leave it to Him — He knows the time of seed-time
and growth-time and fruit-time both in space-time and continent-time
— Baba, thou sun of the gold of the spear and its widening and healing.

Turn in yourself, John — bring back your eyes fond man
from restless visioning. What is it to you that an eye is furtive,
a lip derisive? that speech is ruined and no eyes' lightning
indites the pages of books in lovely verse? Become in your seeing, blind;
in your hearing, deaf — or ever the lovely tide of spring will find you
lip-clinging to a clod of earth and your eyes stretched in an empty sky.

Only a deep Cloud of a Man can rain rains over parched earth.
My gods are diminishing ... Since you are a jealous God,
one lovely in vanity of Alone-selfness, let the Mill-of-you
grind *this* to flour for the hungry-of-you — or let their hunger
grow into a crop of hunger so that they
will the more seek you, and cast this as dust to the wind.

Or, when the grinding is done either to flour or dust, give me a word
a lovely singing word in my mouth, some honey-word, some wine-word
to utter in singing — not for many but for thou in my ear
to delight in; so that my ear may aid mine eyes to fix themselves
only on your dear Form: a singingness of a word —
the lovely word of your Name, thou beloved One, you.

Become unstuck, God, in your entrancement in this which is called me
so that your own love for yourself may be released in a clear stream.
Why do you allow yourself to fall into error, attaching yourself
to everything you see through these eyes? You are the ever-free
blissful One — I am the veil between yourself and you. Tear this veil
which is between us — but if you cannot, ask BABA to do it for you.

Ho, the nothingness of the Nothing which is the things of thingness
contained in the Everything! Nothing am I, and Everything art Thou
my beloved, lovely, and loveliness itself. Ho, what a Box of tricks
you are, Krishna-Baba! Ho, but you are the compassionate One himself,
Buddha-Baba; the most-Shepherd of the flocks of the world, Jesus-Baba;
the long shadowing spear and singing bow One, Rama-Achilles-Baba.

But I would like to be the most-least of a nothing of your servant
and dither about cleaning shoes and carrying water in the ambrosial
dawn hours — by God I would, Baba! It gets a bit irksome
waiting for your word, for you to SAY something,
and this blasted mirk of a black pitch of a night which is not
a dark night but just, as said, a black bitch of a night.

Ho, the nothingness of the Nothing which is the things of thingness
in everything! Nothing am I, but Everything art thou my beloved,
lovely and loveliness itself — you, Lord and dear Child of yourself,
Zeus-Bambino-Baba. But a little love, a little love
injected into us could not altogether be frowned upon as miracle-making,
although it would be a miracle if the injection "took".

But it is no good talking to you, Baba — you are just too-much love.
Whatever we say, you just smile with your smile of divine kindness
as much as to say, "Ho, these children of mine, Myself,—
why did I ever wake up and start singing?" This singing of your smile
stretching out and supporting the nothingness of us-of-the-Nothing.
Oh, and the Dawn-song of His mouth.—I only hope I am still around then.

It's no good talking to One who is the SAYING of the say which one says,
because he doesn't listen because he knows exactly what he is going to
    say.—
Tired and tired am I of myself. For the wide expanse of the sky
of your bosom I cry. Awake in my heart that I may love you with service—
or else be dust before your feet: anything but this not-even-nothing,
nor a place in your Everything; something, O my Child and my Father.

The stars weep, and you have compassion on them in their dew to the
    grass
and the wheatfields; the sun sinks in his shame, and you cover him
with hiding night; but my tears laugh at me and my shame is naked
    before me.
The prayers of the ant and the flame-loving moth are you answering,
and the heavy earth-turning are you guiding with infinite care.—
A song in your praise, or a mute adoration, is not much of an asking.

And there will come the time of your lovely Speaking and your Leaving,
and my going and returning and waiting and emptiness and unlovely
earth under my feet, and wide, wide sky Somewhere you will be.—

And the mother will be answering her child and the loved one
her lover with moon and star glint of love-eyes, Baba —
Baba — God — Sun of earth and Rains of all growing.

Not only can I not sing of you, my beloved, but I have no place
in your work. A lame cur around the streets and backdoors of houses
am I who was once a cattle dog whose teeth were respected. Dog
I would be, but at your heels, Baba, to trot in your dust,
and at camp-fire at night lie a little way off watching your every move,
and when you lay down, myself to follow you again in dream.

But I remember your "Am I not enough" to Abu Sa'id, both at the time
when the people praised him, and when they voided their filth on him.
I remember your utter kindnesses and the hem of your dress in my hand
and your saying, "I am always with you," and your own always-rejection.
The well set mill grinds the wheat small — and you
are the King and the King's Son on earth who pays for us all.

But no — it is not any that reject me: myself rejects me that I may become
acceptable to Him. And just as dog I had to be on my way up to man,
so dog I must become on my way back to myself — Baba, Thou sower
and reaper and grinder ! Thou sifter and again-ear-grower
in each speck of flour ! Surely you are in your loving-kindness
tying up my tongue with the same cords you are cutting away from my
     heart.

You are the great Undoer, so that what shall be done shall be done.
The Remover who brings forward, the Stupifier who makes intelligent.
The Wind that levels the young wheat that the stalks may grow strong
in the sun; while you during the days of its growing
attend other else, and whet with your eyes the scythe of its reaping —
Thou lovely one ! Thou faithless one of all faith !

Thou stonecutter and gemcutter ! Thou potter and breaker of pots !
Thou upturner and returner ! Thou upheavaller and leveller !
Thou bender of what is straight, and Thou straightener of the bent !
Thou Baba ! Thou lovely-Woman and glory-Man and Child ! Thou
     moon-night,
Thou star-night, Thou dawn swept of stars, Thou morning of sun !
Thou alone-doer, Thou adorable and adored — Thou us, Thou
     only-alone-Self !

Thus was John Kerry complaining and praising—for complaint is praise inasmuch as complaint is attachment, and praise is complaint because praise is separation. And he was recognizing that this was the beginning of those subtractions, the sum-total of which would be the subtraction of him from himself. "When the five sheaths are subtracted Atman alone remains. Sivoham, Sivoham—I am EXISTENCEKNOWLEDGEBLISS.

Cease, cease—
      "Swallow Thy Breath Every Moment."

God in the Beyond-Beyond state is likened to a soundless, shoreless Ocean.

The "Whim" of God for knowledge of Himself ("Who am I?") manifested as Sound.

This Oceanic Sound is of God and is God and contains, and is, His experience of Power, Knowledge, Bliss.

The emergence of this Sound through what is called the "Om-Point" or Its Creative Utterance produced the worlds of Mind, Energy and Matter.

This Primal Oceanic Sound is the Root of all forms and creatures and men and they are continuously connected with It and derive their life from It.

When one closes one's lips and expresses sound a "m-m-m" is produced.

This "m-m-m" is the foundation or ground of all spoken words and contains all feelings as when it expresses pain and anguish or joy and happiness, or all thought when expressed during thought and is capable of containing the whole of a question and its answer.

This "m-m-m" is a "drop" of faint sound of the Oceanic Sound, the "M-m-m" or "Word" of God separated from the Ocean by seven shadows of separation.

If the whole physical universe was a huge bell, the sound of it in comparison with Sound of the Oceanic Sound would be as the furthermost point of audibility of an ordinary bell.

This sound-drop is not different from the Oceanic Sound—it is that Ocean and can never be anything but Ocean — but it experiences itself as a drop because of separation.

This separation is not a separation by division, but a separation through impression.

(As words are expressions of this drop—"m-m-m" separated from the Oceanic "M-m-m", so are sense actions expressions and experiences removes from Oceanic Experience: seeing and seen from Oceanic Sight, hearing and heard from Oceanic Hearing, smelling and scent, tasting and flavour, touching and touch from corresponding Oceanic Faculties.)

This Original Oceanic "M-m-m" is called Brahm-Nad (Sound or "Word" of God) or Unhud-Nad (Limitless Sound or "Word").

It is continuous and is the eternal Root and continuous Cause of all causes and effects.

It experiences All-power, All-knowledge and All-bliss; but the drop- "m-m-m", although of the same "substance" and not in any way different from the Oceanic-"M-m-m", and although continuously connected with

It, feels, because of its separation through seven shadows of separation, most weak, most ignorant and most unhappy — even though at times it asserts strength, knowledge and happiness.

In this present age when words, through accumulation and accretion, have become meaningless and all My previous words in the form of Precepts are neglected and distorted, I maintain Silence.

When I break My silence and speak, it will be this Primal Oceanic "M-m-m" which I will utter through My human mouth.

And because all forms and words are from this Primal Sound or Original Word and are continuously connected with It and have their life from It, when It is uttered by Me It will reverberate in all people and creatures and all will know that I have broken My silence and have uttered that Sound or Word.

The effective force of this Word in individuals and their reaction to It will be in accordance with the magnitude and receptivity of each individual mind.

And the reaction will be as instantaneous and as various as the reaction of people in a room through which a cobra suddenly and swiftly passes, when some would nervously laugh, some lose control of their bowels and some feel great courage or reasonless hope and joy.

MEHER BABA

Book III — *God's Speaking*

the question which Reality asked Itself
and the beginning of illusion and its end

Once God, that Great Being,
Whose nature is Existence, Knowledge and Bliss, slept.
He was like a man in deep sleep
Who *is*, but does not know that he is.
He had no knowledge of His knowledge nor experience of His bliss.
He was like a still, shoreless Ocean which no wind or wave
Moved upon. There was nothing but Him.
There were no stars nor sun nor earth nor anything.
All things were within Him; but since He slept,
They also were asleep, unformed and unmanifest.

All knowledge of Himself and of all things were in Him,
But He did not know that He knew.
Then there surged within Him the desire (Whim) to know
Who He was; and He spoke within Himself the First Speech,
"Who am I?" And with the utterance of this First Speech
All things in their potentiality came forth from Him.
But all things are Nothing; and so the universe of stars and suns
Is nothing. Nothing is included in His Everything
But is nothing in itself. But at this time, since He did not know
His Knowledge, He did not know that Nothing was nothing at all.

Each thing He brought forth out of Nothing and caused to exist
In seemingness He, great Only Being, thought He was!
He created stone; thought He was stone; lived as stone
Millions of years, and then said, "Something other am I."
He created vegetation; thought He was vegetation; lived as vegetation
Millions of years, and then said, "Something other am I."
He created in turn worms and reptiles, fishes, birds and animals,
And in turn thought He was, and lived as each, of these.
Then He created Man, and said, "This is sufficient for all My require-
     ments.
I know Myself who I am, because this is in My own Image, Myself.

As man He loved his loves and suffered his loves —
Sunbeat and rain-hail, dew of love;
Whirl-pool and dark wave and threatening rocks; warm-swirl
Of the surf's back-rush round the ankles, and fine sand
Suspended like worlds in the water; salt on eyes and mouth.
Taste of salt on her mouth, and the moon
Come up huge and yellow. Warm honey of kisses,
Warm honey with slight salt. And the pounding of Earth-shaker

Poseidon; and dream-sleep, and the breeze
In the dawn stirring a wisp of her lovely hair.

And the night of moon ended, and the honey
Eaten of her mouth and the stars of her eyes
Fled back into the wells where of sky, and the sun
Come up again in clear sky or murk
Of another day; and the setting out on wash of dark wave
Along hammered streets lined
With open mouths and protruding tongues of Kali
Licking victims and votaries into blast-furnaces,
Goose-stepping them
To the rhythm of type-writer keys.

His loves loved and joyed and suffered, stored and remembered,
Sifted and sorted and evaluated through his many-lives
Till he takes his stand in the flood mightily
And suffers the flood and turns the weight of its waters
To break through the pass of the encircling mountains onto the plains
Of Troyland or Kurukshetra, turns it
Against the massed shields and spears and nodding forest of plumes
And the sudden rifles and hurled destruction and carried death,
Charging himself with impetuous valour in
Unheard of feats of courage and endurance.

No longer can he be counted a man, but is a hero
Unthinkably great and unimaginable in feats
With the weapons of pent waters in his hands and the roar of waters
In his soul. But also great is the enemy.
If he falls he dies a hero's death, and the battle-maidens
Bear him to a hero's reward. But if he sustains the war
And bears on gloriously, and God and his Guru guard him
And pour into his soul divine grace and into his limbs
Unmatchable strength he wins to the first circle
Of the seven-circled citadel of God.

Here he rests, and enjoys the perfumes of paradise
Until the Master, watchful and benign, urges him gently on,
And he mounts to the second shining circle and enjoys
Heavenly music. And again the Master urges on
And he arrives at the third circle of infinite light.
Now if the gentle Murshid urges on again,

Half way across the wide plain of that plane lies Enchantment —
But if he holds steadily to the Master's Name and vision
Of His lovely face he passes the danger
And arrives at the fourth circle of this Way.

Here the powers which tempted Buddha and Jesus in the wilderness
Are ranged against him, nor God nor any man
Save God as fully manifest as a Man perfect in love and power
Can help him — only by the Perfect Master's perfect mercy
Can these powers be held in check,
And the fifth glorious circle won; or turned
And directed towards universal good, thus
Bringing him straightway to the sixth circle
Where he sees God,
His own very Self, face to face continuously.

Now begins the game of love in earnest, to which
The flight of nights of earth-moon and thundering wave
On white beach and stars of eyes and honeyed mouth
And delicate wisp of hair in sudden breeze was apprenticeship
To forgetfulness and service. This is the love
Which only the verses of God Himself or His perfect saints
Can hint us towards — deafness and sightlessness and the wasted frame
And tears: God as a man worshipping God as God,
And God as God loving Himself in a man. And so,
Till He tears the final veil between Him and Himself and answers
His question "WHO AM I ?" with "I AM MYSELF."

_____

Once God slept. And there surged within Him the Urge,
The Whim to know Himself. And He asked Himself
"Who am I ?" and He was objectified to Himself
As opposite to Him, experiencing contrariety
And so disrupting His indivisible poise and eternal tranquillity
And causing in Him experience of impression which was gross, solid —
Himself as separate from Him, finite as opposite to Infinite.
He became conscious, by impression, not of Himself as eternal,
Infinite Self, but of finiteness which, in turn, necessitated form
Seed of contrariety sown by the reverberation of the First Urge.

And He built for Himself a house of stone — not of stone walls
But solid stone — and sat down in it; and because of the closeness
Of stone thought (though without act of thinking) He was stone —
He the eternally free and Only-Existent-One thought He was stone.
But after ages and cycles of this imprisonment
The heat of His desire for Self-knowing melted the stone
And He was freed from imprisonment in stone, but retained
The impressions of stoneness and with these impressions of most solidness
Built for Himself a more commodious house in which
To experience solidness with greater freedom.

This house was iron. And because of its closeness,
Identified Himself with iron and sat
In iron-sitting for ages and cycles — though not so long,
Since iron melts quicker than stone — and this house, too,
Dissolved away. And, using as materials the impressions
Impressioned in consciousness, He built His next house,
Of thick vegetation of mosses and grass
And twining creepers and trees growing thickly. But these,
Though green with sap, burned quickly and His consciousness
Was free of entanglement of dreaming vegetation.

And He opened His eyes to surrounding flesh — worm-flesh
And fish-flesh and bird-flesh and beast-flesh, and last,
Man-flesh. And man-flesh was thin flesh and consumed easily
In the Fire, but desirable above all other forms of flesh;
And so each time the Fire, now identified as love, burned down
One house He quickly built another for His man-experiencing,
So sweet with joy and pain. Man-house and woman-house —
House well-built and strong, jerry-built, designed
In beauty or ugliness; — He the householder — loved, unloved;
Progressing, standing still or falling back in the press of "I".

Loving his loves and suffering his loves — breaking down (death)
And building up again (birth) innumerable houses for His requirement
Of innumerable experience. And between each casting off
(Accompanied by groans and sweats and hopes from priest
And fears from prospect, clinging back and sundering on)
And new assuming, through mother-pains and blood
And hopes and anguish neglected or comforted, heaven
Or hell according to deeds, desires and accomplishments;

Where he sorted out, discarded or accepted values
Of human-beingness — paid pains for "sin", delights for "virtue".

Never arriving at that hidden equipoise which if got
Would finish the infernal see-saw of up-good, down-bad
And back where yer come from to another body because
That's tha way yer want it, although really yer don't.
Equipoise — balance ! — the calm and patient sweat
Of Adepts on the path to Truth — what chance
A bloke got *without a body* attached to solid earth,
Or some fixed, luminous star to hold to, trying to juggle
The Scales of relative value, trying to assess the inertia
Of the Pendulum and hold it midway, six o'clock exact !

But, as the earth-nights of moon and stars of eyes and cool breeze
Over the still-warm sands curling a wisp of hair
Across her brow which nourished his vision, and the roar
Of the surf of earth-shaker Poseidon pointing his impulse
(Pulse of Life-force) to More-than-himself, to distance,
Was apprenticeship to forgetfulness and service by which
He would become — Oh, in what ages and cycles to come ! — a lover of God,
So all this fumbling with scales betwixt breaking up
And again building of innumerable houses was schooling for the day
When would be revealed to him the eternal values of Truth.

Going and coming: demolishing with fire one house
And building another with bricks of impressions baked in the fire —
Till he takes his stand in the flood and turns the waters
To control the fire; or grasps Fire in two hands wet
With weeping, and worshipping its glowing countenance
Moves It to burn the rubbish in the house; or seeks the Master
Bright beyond Fire's brightness, moist-eyed with floods
Of beneficence and mercy and offers Him the sin
Of vice and virtue of householding — offers Him his-bricks-of
Himself to be pounded back into clay for remodelling.

Takes his stand and stops playing the role — stops
Walking about the house admiring it, picking up nick-nacks
From the shelves, dusting and stroking and acknowledging them
As worth and placing them back in just-right places;
Looking out from the sitting-room windows at the view and garden

Thinking, a shrub there, some so and so flowers there — I
The householder; turning back into the room, considering
His face — a few grey hairs, figure — a bit too much,
In the mirrors; and turns on himself coldly or savagely
And deliberately opens the door and leaves it to whomso to loot and enjoy.

But whatever — comes at last the ripening through loves and unloves,
Swift joys and slow pain, sure grasp and shaking hand,
Ripened to indifference and alertness and he takes his stand
In the current of comings and goings; and next time he comes, he comes
With transparent residual impressions for building material
And builds him his next-last house through which from outside
Light shines, and he loses himself in dreaming light.
And goes in light and weighs light and returns
With materials of Light and builds a house of Light
And meditates Light, becomes Light and never again returns.

Once God slept. And awoke; and journeyed in immense journeying
Through stone and metal and green of earth and worm
And fish and bird and animal and assumed Man-shape,
And as Man loved his loves and suffered his loves and died
To his loves and was born to them again and again —
Repeating each time the folly of "I" and "you", "yours"
And "mine", linking securely the links of the evil chain.
A man — sunlight of eyes and pastures of sweet lips;
Dark night and the cruel wave curling beneath.—The Road?
The Road? Himself the Road — love, and the grace of the Master.

Dropped last-role state, called heaven and hell —
Pleasure and suffering intensified through lack of dampening flesh.
Hell is hot or cold or hot and cold according
To heat of desires and coldness of love — but world,
Himself, is Fire which ever heats the crucible of forms
In which is melted the impressions of flesh and bone and brain
Back to their origins of earth; Fire which, after the clay
Is moulded again as bricks for heart's next desire,
Bakes them to hardened form for soul's next enterprise:
Himself, brickmaker, fire; house-builder and householder.

74

Heaven and hell — place of attempted scales-balancing
From which, again-coming and assuming another form
To play another role upon the stage of world-seeming; remembering
Nothing of the last part or endless list of performances,
The new role in accordance with the shapes of ardencies and sloths,
The qualities and direction of greeds and altruisms — the means
Of spending these impressions and in the spending taking up
Fresh debt to try and balance in dropped-body state:
The present role, a bark and growl, or a singing of sweet waters
In sunlight over crystal sand, according to intent and vehicle.

Vehicle of gross-body. Grossness is finiteness —
Seed of separation — to which consciousness clings
While Self longs for return. Consciousness clings to the earth
Like a child to its mother, while soul peeps out from behind her skirt
To fresh adventure of play; or from security of warmth
Kneels before winter window dreaming of spring and sun
And vaguely voyaging. Consciousness clings to the earth,
To its body which is every moment passing away and returning
And says, This is my home, myself; while soul skies-dreams
Journeys and performances unhindered by body's weight.

Never coming to terms with it: never for long
Undividedly enjoying residence in earth and form's
Promises: never holding beyond the duration of the glass
Wine's *taste*; beyond the duration of the kiss, forgetfulness;
Beyond the night, release: moon of beauty — and then, harsh sun
Of day and baked or frozen lands or narrow streets, and fears.
Resident in earth: house-building; bridge building to beyond
Earth's boundaries — and the unseen bridge: and reviewing unskilfully
Experience of earth-residence —"good" against "bad", "bad" against
     "good"—
Equipoise — engrossment, and "falling" to birth to experience *that*
     engrossment.

Till he meets the blissful, compassionate Master and takes his stand
In the flood, in the currents of himself and says in himself,
Enough has been far too much. And willingly and reverently
And with joy high-hoped bows before that One of wisdom and light
Saying, Teach me and help me. And he, the great One
Who crossed and returned again over the ocean of fire

And waters, this Odysseus of voyaging, twice-born after visiting
The land of Death without dying and so dead to life, reaching Home
Where his treasure was and filling his ship with abundant gold
And returning over the trackless sea to succour famished men, says:

Fear not, my child, My lover — there is a Way through the sea
Of appearance in which you are swirled, a method
Of stopping the whirling wheel of rebirth, a means whereby
The foundations of your present house may be shattered
And no more built. For every knot tied there is an untying,
For every pain a remedy, for every ignorance a replacement
With knowledge. Ancient is this Knowledge, so ancient,
That God on His first arrival back into Himself after His
Same journey you are making, knew it and brought it down
To earth as first Avatar — so ancient, yet ever wondrously new.

And sings to him with sweet voice the deathless story of Self's journeying:
Of the Beyond Beyond state in which He slept in vast tranquillity
Like to a shoreless, waveless ocean — Knowledgeless.
And His awaking with desireful curiosity to know Himself which brought
        about
He leaving Himself and wandering in ignorant identifications
As stone, as metal, as vegetation, as worm, fish, bird,
Animal and man through countless ages; and then as Man,
Birth after birth millions of times in which He experienced
Being man and woman, rich and poor, foolish and wise, healthy and sick
And all the possible opposites engendered by separation.

How He took His stand and fought the wars of returning
And returned — now with all-Knowledge, all-Power and still Bliss.
And came down again as Saviour to man-selves of Himself —
His various Avatars, each one unique and lovely, perfectly Himself:
Of Zarathustra bringer of the sacred fire of love and pure
Intelligence; Rama the archer whose arrows were shining light;
Abraham the pure who taught man to worship One God;
Krishna the player of divine music in human hearts;
Buddha the tender who showed men the passingness of life;
Jesus the only real ascetic; and Mohammed who lived with men.

Sings to him the Song of Wayfaring, the adult occupation —
Melting his heart with its sweetness and inspiring
His soul with its possibility. Then gives to him the precious word

To be his sword to cut through the hosts of himself — the hosts
Of vast exile nourished by the moon and bright-foamed sea
And stars of eyes and horizons of brow and wells of sweet lips
And sun, clear, or in murky sky, and hammered streets;
A sword to slay the great Beasts of far past, to cut
Himself free from entrancement on the dazzling planes; and go on, back
To the Master — He to cut the last veil between him and Himself.

Once, God slept. And awoke
Half waking into dreaming. And spread out
The creation as a great tree, its roots
In the Nothing of His dream,
Its branches and leaves and fruits in the Nothingness
Of appearance.
It is called the Tree of Knowledge
Because by it God came to Self-knowledge —
For before He ate of its fruits, He
Even God, knew not Himself.

The Tree of Knowledge through experience
Of "good" and "evil", its sweet and bitter
Fruits. And because God ate
Of these fruits and *became* God,
They are not forbidden men. The Tree of Knowledge
Which is the Tree of Life kept living by the rivers of Necessity
And Compassion and Wisdom and infinite Love — the Sole Growth
Blossoming universes and Man: the Tree on which
God crucified Himself in limitation; on which
Men crucify themselves, each other, and dear God.

Tree, which He spread out from His single breath of inquiring.
Tree, sap of light, fruits of
Stone-fruits and metal-fruits and tree-fruits
And worm-fruits and fish-fruits and bird-fruits and beast-fruits
And man-fruits — fruits which nourished Great God
On His journey for Knowledge; and which, through eating,
He became. And overcame.
And became the Energy which grew the Tree.
And became the Mind which gives it existence.
And became God Which He always was.

Tree, Wishing Tree which bears
The fruit of every desire — fruit which contains within it
Thirst and fresh desire; tree into which
Slouch-hatted, one-Eyed Odin thrust the Sword
Of heroes and battle — earth-battle; planes-battle:
Tree of fragrances of nights and moon
And washed beach for bed and eyes' wells and brow's dream,
And wave-lap against side of boat moored
For journeying; and of sun coming up in chattering street,
Or jewel-sitting in glory on distant mountain peak.

Dream Tree of Dreamed-creation, whose waving branches
Are the Dance of God which makes us crazy and sets us housebuilding
And demolishing and again-building: Annamayakosa; Pranamayakosa;
Manasmayakosa with Vigñanamayakosa and Anandamayakosa.

>   Nirmanakaya
>   Sambodhakaya
>   Dharmakaya.

Light. Light. The light from the Master's lips
Is the Scriptures; from His hands the Path-setting;
From His eyes the tearing of veils — the ruin of the last-built house.

Build we our houses with bricks of impressions, cement of desire
Mixed with tears.— Build we our houses —
So well-pleased so well-pleased —
Come into my house wipe your feet first please wipe your feet —
Sit we and talk we smile and be gay —
No God-talk please or allusion-to-Way talk —
God-talk and Way-talk is crank-talk not tea-talk —
Gay-talk for you for me talk
With sun reduced sun of venetian blinds
In this house of me-house built by me.

Master-builder ! Master-builder ! — the One
Who built this lousy little house builds also universes:
Spins suns in burning, hums earths
Around them; spaces them in spacelessness,
Times them in timelessness and orders the time
Of their ceasing from turning. Master-builder, Master-builder —
Self the creator, Self the sustainer, Self the destroyer; Self
The Mirror-maker of Image of Himself.—Little householder,

Bright are your tears of happiness and sorrow, portion self-gotten.
Pitiable your bed and table and bowed walk — pitiable, and glorious.

Light of the physical sun with which is the moon
And curved shape and solid form — frame for Art:
Light of the divine Sun which lights the forms in infinite appearance
Of reality. Man is God in man-shape suffering enjoyment and suffering
Self-separation; divine Sun weeping veils to cover Him from Self
And crying to sun for light, to earth for sustenance, to moon
For beauty: All-giver become beggar before the doors of nothingness;
Dreamer absorbed in dreaming trying to shake Himself free
From the web of dream — to discern the Real, to choose
The hard choice of the Light-road forking at each step.

Journeys; dies, and takes birth; journeys until tired,
And rests and considers the outcome of journeying; holds
What he has acquired, for so long. and examines it,
And discards the trash: dies; takes birth; examines
And discards; begins dying in love-death of rebirth in love-life —
The house (so carefully built) crumbling bit by bit,
Before the same fire which baked its bricks, to dust
Under His glorious feet — to sing His praise or silently adore,
Or for His wind to blow anywhither
Or be remoulded into useful Self-shape in His service.

Takes his stand, at last takes his stand and rejects
The Moon-road to rebirth in form's delight and pain
Of nights of cool breeze over warm sands curling
A wisp of fragrant hair across brow dreaming unseen light,
And near thunder of Poseidon's horses on blue paddock of ocean;
And dawns; and disastrous days of ambition realized or thwarted —
The Moon-road to lovely form and fear and hope.
And takes the Sun-road, the death-road to immortal Self —
Unborn, undying abodeless Being, Knowledge, Bliss
Who built no houses, only dreamed a dream.

Once God slept — untroubled by shadow of dream, unknowledged
With knowledge of good and evil, without knowledge even of Himself
Being infinite Knowledge. From sleep He awoke and marched out

And unfurled worlds of finiteness (hardness of contrariety)
And planted them up through the seven Kingdoms as banners
Of false conquest. And stood and took His stand in Himself-flood
And turned it back and won back to Himself — stripping Him
Of not-Himself as He went: and arrived glorious in real conquest
From Where He started and slept AWAKE-Sleep of Emptiness
Filled with "I am God"— Power, Knowledge, Bliss: the Goal.

Book IV — *The Steps to His Feet*

abandoning illusion for Reality

So must be prepared the ground
for the sowing, for the entering
of the seed of light in one's earth.
The seed of man is the gathered light of form,
the seed of light is the grace of the Perfect Master.

The first is coupled with death; the second
is the cause of immortality. Following the moon path
is rebirth; following the track of the sun
the wheel of birth is broken — man is reborn in the Deathless,
never to return except as a Perfect Master.

Worshipping the gods of thy god, the gods of gadgets and guns
one is born again where the burden may be re-assumed,
where the fright and the frustration may be again enjoyed;
worshipping with surrenderance and love the name and form of God
to God one comes when it is the Whim of the Perfect Master.

Suffering birth again and again, and never learning
that ourselves of our desires and hopes
exist not, but arose out of Nothing — Nothing,
held loosely in Everything's hand as a game for Its knowledge
that It comes at long last to the condition of a Perfect Master.

Held in Its hand as a ball and tossed
and caught and tossed by a man marking the pleasure
of his marksmanship, or as a mirror in a lovely woman's hand
advising her of her loveliness, is the world of forms
and births in the hand of the Perfect Master.

Thus, the sunbeat and wave roll and breaking of dream-joys
and dream-pains; and the eyes washed,
or sealed with new pain — the one adored melting
into one's outline of desiring, or hardening into bitter pain, until
we of ourselves melt into the eyes and love of the Perfect Master.

The clearing of the ground for the sowing, for the entering,
is the unlearning of learning — for learning
is your rubbish heap of conceit. For this,
in the first place, Prometheus-Agni brought down
the heavenly fire by order of the Perfect Master.

But some mind-impressions do not burn, and for these
Siva brought down the waters of the Ganges
to drown them; to create on earth
a reservoir of tears for lovers — rivers
divine-Ocean bearing according to the will of the Perfect Master.

And some neither burn nor drown, but must be strangled
to death. Hence it is said, "Swallow
thy breath every moment." But this is not possible
unless by the gift of divine love one is strangled for sight
of Him — the gift of the Perfect Master.

To unlearn all one has learned! a bitter
swallowing; a chasmal yawping before one's feet;
a yawping yawning; a wide widdy
to hang fat-necked conceit — impossible
without the guidance of the Perfect Master.

So it is said, "One moment in the company of a saint
is worth a hundred years of penance and prayer," and
as Baba pointed out, Jelaluddin was talking only about saints —
how much magnified when related
to the being of God in the person of the Perfect Master!

All written words are dead until you bring them to life.
But the life you give them
will be your own image of falseness,
not Truth's: Truth is contained only
in the life-giving word of the Perfect Master.

It is better to read than gossip;
it is better to meditate than read;
it is better to love than meditate; but
since you are already trapped in the coils of mental convulsions,
read the books of the saints and "God Speaks" by the Perfect Master.

And serve other than self since self
is the veil between oneself and Self. But the hindrance
to this is delight in praise and resentment
of blame and love of expressing these two — unless
directed according to the instructions of the Perfect Master.

Or deny the world and oneself
and in utter solitude regardless
of food and wet or dry and cold or hot
fix one's mind wholly and undividedly on the formula "I am God",
until He appears in the form of the Perfect Master.

Or practise the moral law and accept
the responsibilities sowing and reaping
has apportioned one — the bones of religion
to pick and rattle, until the round of time
brings one round to fortune of sight of the Perfect Master.

The moral law — first make peace with thy brother.
But pitiful indeed is one who says, "First the affairs of the world,
then the path to God." Easy the path, he thinks!
The weight of the world will anchor his feet and never
will he find the path to the door of the Perfect Master.

Pitiful the one who because of a dream
of an angel visiting him or Christ speaking,
imagines he is on the path. Sunk in a stupor
on the seashore watching a ship passing —
but not on its deck the lovely Person of the Perfect Master.

Pitiful the one who says, "Alone I will do it."
He has not heard, "The Way is strewn with the bones
of hundreds of thousands who thought thus." Or "Though you be a lion,
come in under the shade of this Palm-tree"—
sayings of warning because of the compassion of the Perfect Master.

Twaddling and twittering are they, snooking and sniting,
hopping nervously puss-purring and piddle-puddling,
while ranging the hills, His glorious mane sweeping the earth
and the Roar of His throat gathering itself for the day of His
lovely utterance, is the Lion of God, Christ, the Perfect Master.

Nor follow the way of the rice-christians, the ones
in it for the handout, who reckon Heaven
is a ready built home on a lottery-won allotment and God
a cow to be tethered on the back lawn for milking —
mean men who refuse the lovely song-call of the Perfect Master.

Nor follow those who close their eyes and behold themselves
infinitely desirable; and repeat the formulae of their own names,
or breathe — on the inbreath magnifying themselves,
on the outbreath exuding self-stench — while even
the dumb earth swims in the perfumed breath of the Perfect Master.

Nor dung your eyes and ears with pigments and words
and sounds of seeming relation, blinding your eyes
to the lovely Model of Man and your ears
to His singing. Nor theories nor works will avail
to imprint in your hearts the Form and Message of the Perfect Master.

The spiritual path is the natural occupation of adults;
unconcern is the prerogative of children. The child
came here out of curiosity, but the child became a man
in order to experience in the world (his own body)
the grace of the Perfect Master.

— Oh, in the dawn I heard the news being bandied about,
"Today is being spread the feast for the Tavern-keeper's son."
I would sweep the floor of the tavern with my eyelashes
if there was any chance of being invited
to a drinking bout with the disciples of the Perfect Master.

And I heard (in my dreaming, which, O fool,
I fondly imagine is waking) the sound
of great drops of water splashing, and saw a fountain
glorious in the sun, and knew (or was told)
"These are the tears of compassion of the Perfect Master."

Decked in tinsel of riches and position
a man is a caricature of *likeness* unto God,
an idol of self-worship. Adorned with divine qualities
natural in a man, he declares
his true sonship to the Perfect Master.

Material ambition is delusion that acquisition is security —
but what the world calls security is proved
no-security because it rests upon that
which is changing and passing and not upon love
which is the root and being and crown of the Perfect Master.

86

Self is not any of the conditions or qualities it imagines —
nor "somebody" nor "nobody" nor "accomplished" nor "unaccomplished".
All these are impressions impressioning mind, vehicle of Self.
The natural condition of Self is love — its demonstration
is the being and life and acts of the Perfect Master.

Remember the Love of your loves. All are pleased
with the gift but few praise the Giver
until another snatches away the gift. Behind the sun-days
and the moon-nights is the glory and gentleness
of the Sun and the Moon of the Perfect Master.

Beneath the cry and complaining for position and honour
is the cry and weeping of the soul for Self-established Existence.
Beneath the fret and restriction is the restlessness
and the bond-breaking and the going-forth from oneself
to Self Who is none other than the Perfect Master.

There is music struck with the hand or laboured
to voice-utterance; there is the unstruck music of the heart
and the soul's clear and effortless singing. There is
the written verse and the hand-painted picture; and the painting
of the soul in *likeness* of the Perfect Master.

September of the passing year, and Eternal Spring;
soft winds laden with the orchard's sweetness, and the Breeze
coming from the garden of the Beloved — a choice
easy for the planesmen, but hard for us
who have not yet found favour with the Perfect Master.

The pious and the materialists have their reward
and the perfume-seller on the street corner has occasionally
the eye of love returning his bright glances —
but we who have no love nor piety nor hope of rewards
nor work in the service of the Perfect Master?

So He has advised us to leave it to Him,
as aforetime He told us to take no thought for tomorrow.
Tomorrow means still hope, and He already
has been hopeless and helpless on the roads of the world that we
may become helpless and hopeless of all save the Perfect Master.

Unlearn your learning, unhope your hopes, unlove
your loves; nothingness is becoming to those
arisen from Nothing. Clear some ground for Love,
Love, the entire forgetter, the only rememberer,
the Chastener and Cherisher — the Perfect Master.

And seek the glorious One, thyself, unborn
undying, unfretted and undismayed; thyself,
Creator of heaven and earth; unloved, unhated,
but Love perfect and existent alone in Self:
thyself, in the form and being of the Perfect Master.

Seek His love, or ever the dark wave shall bear you
in fiercest sunbeat of days and terrible
loneliness of nights, nor flag nor friend to greet you —
utter night, and the dark wave curling above you. Seek his love
and forgiveness while yet He is here in form of the Perfect Master.

Clearing the ground is erasing the impressions of the mind.
Impressions are the veils between ourselves and Truth.
When they are erased "Self stays in His native condition"—
Self, the beyond-God of love from where we once came;
the here-God of redemption in the person of the Perfect Master.

The Perfect Master: the Man-God who was a man who became God
Who became a man; the Perfect Master Who is God directly descended
Who takes the wheel of the World-Car from the hands of the
Perfect Masters' No. 1 driver and drives the new Circuit and establishes
correct lap-time — of all Perfect Masters the *Perfect Master*.

The *Perfect Master*, Avatar
    Who is none but God
        Who is the EVERYTHING
Which contains the Nothing
        And His devotee.

Book V — *The God-Man as World Axis and Living Perfection of Art*

the Divine Sun of Reality shining through
the mists of illusion

PART I

Theme:

Art is an act of love in likeness of itself — Spirit
moulding matter into lovely form: God's compassion
as Avatar unto men; and men's devotion to Avatar as God,
by God — for devotion is by grace alone.
Avatar is His own act perfectly:
before His different Names speech retreats in confusion;
before the Living One, the One present on earth in one's life,
one can only say, "O God. O God." And weep; and wait;
wait the round of His time and the poetry of His word
to enform us in likeness and paint us in livingness.
Devotion is winged sacrifice under the shadow of His wings
flying to Him; an arrow crying in the night for dissolution
in love's mark; the dew of morning diamonding His sun
as a necklace for His throat: His act in us for Him.

1
Once men sang purely in the work of their hands,
in the speech of their mouths. They knew
that Avatar and the Perfect Masters were the only God on the earth,
and that the saints were doors to Him.
By God men lived — and His Name wrought their works:
they went not out to labour nor sat down to meat
without song attending. (The left over scraps from their singing
we have gathered into our galleries and libraries to worship or stare at.)
Then spirit faltered, losing its way somewhat
in the darkening lanes of the blood.
And Siva gave a new scripture — His knees
beseeched by lovely Parvati — for men's easement; set
a new light in the ingle in their cottages; gave a new calling
for their speech to call in their hearts.

2
Shone in their hearts in again-Brightness;
lit in their hearts the way of sacrifice, revealing
the ever-Friendliness of God;
shot with His shining arrows into the darkness, establishing
a new sun wherever each pierced the dark;

brought into their hearts again music;
taught pity;
showed them the pilgrim route; and gave them the bride Poverty.
In Buddha, Jesus and Mohammed He was clustered closely,
but a long time from Mohammed to now-Baba—1400 years. Mohammed's
     art
lasted a thousand years of it; for the last four hundred years, drought:
the science of Self dumped in favour of star measurements
and behaviour of atoms; the singing of Avatar's deeds
replaced by soul's sprawl hugged in tightness to itself.

3
After Zarathustra, the light purely again in men's eyes,
brightly between lovers and above the marriage-bed,
and in conversation and contracts. After Abraham, the settled life
in obedience to God's voice, consequently friendship
between men — who had what to fear from whom?
The tent pitched or struck at His word. "I do not bow down
before that which *rises* and *sets*." After the wanderings
of Rama and Sita and Lakshman, the pure dignity
of women established, and brotherliness without jealousy;
Mind (Hanuman) delighting in service,
delighting in solitary meditation and uninterrupted repetition
of God's Name — shining arrows flying
into the sun in the empyrean of heart: each "Rama"
answered by, "Here am I"—Love's dialogue.

4
After Krishna, the singing of Vyasa meditated
and composed in exact likeness of His acts of love;
the singing recitations of the saints; Iliad, Odyssey;
Edda (although not written down until by
Saemund the Wise, 1056-1133) song of His flute
for the first time in the hearts of the North-men; song
self-existent, Moinuddin Chishti; magic-song capable
of lighting lights, Tansen; Mirabai singing her way to God.
After Krishna, the sadhana of dance, demonstrated
by David, Jelaluddin, Chaitanya, Tukaram —
half the world dancing in the Gopi's footsteps;
half the world listening for the notes of His flute, dividing them
into ragas and modes and scales, arranging them into melody-offerings.
After Krishna, Sappho, Ambrose, Qwaali, Bhajan, Flamenco.

5

After Buddha, men loving solitude —"Unless a man set his heart
in order he can in nowise establish the kingdom
of heaven on earth." Hence Saraputti; hence Anuradhapura;
hence Tang painting and poetry; and Hui Neng the thirty-third
in direct descent, tearing up scriptures, and along with other Zen men
delighting in caricaturing one another, banishing solemnity
but taking the job seriously: Shang waiting out in the snow for a week
for interview with his Lordship Bodhidharma and then sending in his
   right hand.
After Buddha, Noh, and tea-drinking, and the proper way to sweep a path;
and Marpa the translater in his old age tramping across the hills for the
"Short-cut Doctrine", and it demonstrated by Thopaga in the wilderness.
After Buddha, the clear reasoning of Socrates; and Sankaracharya
to break the back of a Buddhism NOT taught by Buddha and raise again
the banner of "I am God"; and Pragñanaparamitahridayasutra.

6

After Jesus, John writing perfect poetry; and Peter
made worthy and altogether lovely through terrible remorse of denial —
to whom M. Angelo & Co. made a monstrous monument;
the Egyptian and Syrian deserts carpeted with flowers;
the Seven Golden Odes of Imr Al Qais (even though "Guide to hell")
   and Co.;
and Kailas frescoes. After Jesus, Sun of fourth heaven,
Ploughshare through the garbage-tip of Rome —
short work-span — came Mohammed. After Mohammed,
the pure brothers, masters of heart (saheb-i-dil), and the whole
linked flood of lovely singers in continuance after Krishna:
Abu Bakr, Ali, Ibn 'Arabi, Junaid,
Attar, Abu Sa'id, Hafiz, Jelaluddin,
Chretien de Troyes, Daniel, Ramon Lull, St. John of the Cross,
down to present qwaals at the Baba-Sahavas singing to Baba.

7

After Mohammed, Establisher of Democracy, the cultivation
of the Heart-doctrine was again easy, and men could easily
love men — re-establishment of the sharing-companionship
of the early Christians and carried through
to the time of the great Assisian lover, who, however, was still
calling Mohammed by His former name of Jesus;
Chartres, Granada, the Wandering Scholars,—

pure line of Mohammed's gentleness and generosity.
Singing as of great bells — rhythm of God in the hearts
of men as in the morning of stars and men when the night fled:
stone laid on stone with reverence and care,
carved images of Jesus and Krishna in stone and wood
in their *image*; men great in kingship and vassalage,
learned in the true scripture of love.

8

Men who were not afraid to become "blind in their seeing
and deaf in their hearing", and trust that a Khizr
would guide their feet in the world and instruct them
in the way of knowledge and song: for unless a man
becomes blind he shall not have bright-eyed sight
to trace out the lineaments of love, Avatar's
true form — the sort of sight which enabled Demodocus
to follow Odysseus, and Valmiki, Rama's journey.
Learned men able to read hearts,
and the signs of God in the wind, in the fire,
in the green earth; capable of writing the word love
into the work of their hands, their swordsmanship
and ploughing, their pots in which they drew water and
cooked their food and offered sacrifice to God.

9

The Dark Ages were the ages of light: the Renaissance
was the twilight of our present black night of materialism.
Once, men burnt their desires in the sacred fire
of devotion and austerity, made lovely their lives in His mould,
measured the reach of their hands and the range of their speech
by His word, then purely sang in words and notes and stone
Avatar's deeds — thus pleasing God with works
in likeness of His own creativeness. Then men forgot that
"By association with saints all filth is removed,
"by association with saints the face becomes bright,
"by association with saints pride is effaced,
"by association with saints divine knowledge is revealed."
That "One instant in the company of a saint
is better than hundred years of penances and prayers."

10

The Dark Ages were the Ages of Light. Then men denied the saint in
    them,

and the saint in them died, and the line of the saints
came to an end; and there were no channels by which the flow of truth
could be reflected in men's lives. Renaissance, promise
of freedom from "two-dimensional form"; vision of smoke stacks
behind the eyes, ears twiching in anticipation
of symphony of machines. Spirit took wings —
to the *terra firma* of colonization, to solid commodities
sweated out of the labour-energy of other people
(armies of bees standing in line
sweating out wax of cement and steel) :
colonization, last reach of, establishment of territories
in space from which to dominate the whole earth.

11
Renaissance, power-population expansion,
possible by the sciences; lauded by the arts:
science, which once laid down the steps to Self-realization;
art, which once sang God's likeness in the earth —
now "sciences" making machinery of exploitation,
now "arts" singing the virtues of despoliation.
Forgotten, Conceptual Verities;
forgotten, Intuitional Representation.
The servants and devotees of Truth became
the tools and mouthpieces of gunmen. "Your pride
is to trace your descent from a robber-baron;
our greatest king, to trace his to a forest-sage."
Knights of the Middle Ages and heroes of the Great Ages now hired
        officers;
the great bards and troubadours now verse-jinglers and journalists ...

12
"The sun was setting over Shri Kailas.
I bowed to the four directions, spread
my tiger-skin on the ice, planted my staff on the right
and cried, 'Victory to the Lord, my Master !'
then sat in Siddhasana facing north,
fixing His glorious Image between my eyes.
Cruel winds, bitter cold, snow up to my chest;
but unbounded love defeated these enemies.
On the third day the Lord Dattatreya
in His physical form came to me,
picked me up as a child and caressed me:

Manas merged into Antakarana, Antakarana
into Chitta, Chitta into Buddhi, into Ahamkara;
all into the Satchitananda of the supreme Self."

13
"Without the Name of God no man
comes to that knowledge which is the true knowledge;
without Guru no man can learn the Name of God."
Because Guru is the only God you'll
ever see on this plane — Guru, God's act to men.
"Coming home along the river I passed Sheikh Abu'l Fadl
who glanced at me out of the corner of his eye.
I owe all my perfection to that one glance."
Once men journeyed within themselves until they came
to the source of energy and could control their passions,
now they journeyed outwardly in conquest of the earth;
once dug in their hearts to find the gold of Self,
now in the earth for metals to make aeroplanes and bombs.
Technique of former laid down by Zarathustra, Patanjali.

14
We became enamoured of travel, intoxicated
with the sensation of movement. "Let us hitch-hike to another city."
"Let us go find more oil-wells." "Let us find oil in the ocean."
"Let us build an opera-house." "Let us organize more
appreciation classes, last year 10,000, this year
20,000 must be our goal." "Let us build a big plane,
a rocket-plane and go to the moon." We must go somewhere
where we will not find ourselves.
We were saying: breakfast in London
lunch in Cairo. The Arctic Route
cuts off two hours. We said "diesel" instead of "train"—
diesel is faster than train. "Jet" is faster than "plane".
More time to consider the lily in another's heart?
to watch the leaf-bud and flower putting-forth of our own?

15
The sky-scrapers of New York are the cathedrals of America.
A cathedral is an aspiration, a glory, a peace —
a silence reaching to the Silence which is God.
It is the vertical line from the horizontality of human limitation
to the dimensionless point of human (divine mind) unlimitedness —

the Sushumna of unfolding from the Muladhara to the
Thousand Petalled Lotus in the crown of the head. A cathedral
is a line between man and God studded with gems of adoration.
You should go to New York. You should see culture
stockpiled. You should see the herd of faces which don't smile,
the crowd of eyes which don't laugh; the poor children of the rich
being wheeled in Central Park, buttoned to the eyes from the weak sun.
The skyscrapers of New York are beautiful in their reach to death —
lovely with red tears of undedicate labour.

16

A cathedral is a line in the azure decked
with devotee's tears — a shaft of Siva
glorious in the rising sun. A people whose lives
are lived in faith, who live their lives in their hearts
and offer the work of their hands to the various gods of God
wear their cathedrals lightly — as birds wear the burden
of the morning, as Jetsun Milarepa wore the jewel of illness
presented to him by the Geshe's concubine.
You should see an Indian village. How beautiful, God,
are your villages! how exquisite
are the flowers of children growing out of your dirt.
How beautiful is dirt. The mania for cleanliness
is the fury of those outside the enclosure of intimacy.
They even garden in gloves. Maybe some of 'em wear 'em in bed.

17

God is to be found in the heart of beauty; beauty
is dirt moulded by the hands of the sun and vivified
with His breath. Children and *masts* seek dirt
and in it discover their freedom, as in dust
Majnun found Leila. A *mast* in his dirt
is a challenge to God — a rose in dung challenging the sun,
and the sun electrifies its face in the contours of its own energy,
making ashamed all clean people who come near it.
How lovely is dirt from which emerges
the nightingale of a child's eyes:
dirt in which Krishna played; with which
the child Eknath made images of God; with which
Sri Sankaracharya demonstrated before the unbelievers
the Oneness of God — supremacy of Advaita over Atheism.

18

The curse of the West is its great cities: the glory of India
is its villages. When 80 per cent of a people live in villages
you can't conquer the country — they only
pay their taxes to a bloke with another name.
When 80 per cent of the people live in villages and take God's Name
and listen to Sankirtan you may be sure
of the continuance of the line of saints, and that
the Perfect Masters have picked that place to take birth in.
When the majority of the people herd into the cities
you may be sure that no one any longer
sings or dances or *sees* anything as it *is*,
or "finds the precise word to express the tone of the heart".
When the majority ... and the red wind of pent violence
shakes the atom-plums off the tree ...

19

And there are a number of ed-u-cated Indians
who believe the West is a sort of Buddha-lands of prosperity;
they can even supply calorific data. But one wonders
did they, when they wus gettin' their western ejacation,
ever bother to drive round our slums or visit
a shanty-town or do a few weeks on a process-bench?
or inquire into the fact that a bubble-economy *must* expand
or bust? and take note of the fact
that the breath of the bubble is fear; and that so long
as you keep making guns you have "full employment"?
It is an impressive sight to see giant jaws biting into the earth,
or ribbons of molten metal unwinding light — until you know
that if the jaws lock or the ribbons snap we face unbelievable famine;
and if they go on biting and unwinding, we face certain destruction.

20

The gentleman who commented irritably and apologetically
on a farmer drawing water with bullocks instead of an engine —
"But, of course, he could not afford to buy one"— had not
heard the arithmetical answer of another farmer:
"I have five sons. Yes, with machinery, one son and myself
could do the work. The other four could go into factories and
make the machines so that one son and myself could do the work."
Only a *peasant* could think of such a crazy answer.
Or the high school Headmaster who was confused because

" 'Science' was proving the statements of our great sages
to be wrong — e.g. ninety elements, not five", apparently
hadn't read Widagdha Shikala's questions on how many gods
are there? and Yadnyawalkya's answer
that it all boils down to One God only.

21
But the young chap from Delhi was not confused.
"You needn't think we'll go communist or democratic," he said.
"We've got our own tradition of thousands of years of co-operation."
He has also read the old Books and loves the uniqueness
of Krishna and knows his country's problems and is
a disciple of the Living Master. And the Bhajan-singers
who carry Baba's message from house to house are not confused;
nor the boy with his oxen; nor the girls with their "red earthen pitchers".
Nor was the young airman confused or apologetic—he who was
a living flower of chivalry, courteous, brave,
modest, extremely beautiful; a very perfection of young manhood
who always took God's Name when he sat in the cockpit
and who, when his plane crashed
stood before Baba before the thing happened.

22
Didjer ever notice how haggard the women are getting?
They have to put on their faces more often — because
there's no longer any *men* around. Did it
ever occur to you that a woman needs a man more than space-travel?
They don't want such a terrible lot — a hovel
for their bodies so long as its clean; a house in their hearts
to *discover,* to look around in delight and amazement,
a place of security in which to have their babies.
But by God, if you cheat them with a hovel of a heart
they will hate you with such a hate as will drive you
to build bigger and bigger houses for their bodies,
faster and faster cars which FLOAT instead of clawing the road
on the bends, faster and smoother planes, because
the hurt of their heart is beyond their endurance.

23
Have you ever stopped in the tracks of your progress
and asked who is this other person living with me?
It would be too humiliating to find that that fine brain
which can measure infinitesimal measurements and set

99

armies hacking each other to pieces, is knowledgeless
regarding that wonder called a woman. It takes
a man who does nothing, to know her — a man
who will for Christ's sake stop jigging about like an imbecile,
who will sit down and sweat on a pick and shovel
or a rock drill in his own heart; who will, thread by thread,
discard the filthy rags of himself; who will make a woman
out of himself so that he can take her into himself —
for only in himself will he ever know himself in her:
that he is the veil of her, beyond which, is the sun of the Sun of God.

24

Because you love the indolence which you call "progress"
you made of her a play-toy, first for your body, then for your intellect.
Towards the first, you established the cult of the "petite" and robbed her
of the ability to walk properly and caused her to bear
her children in unnatural pain; toward the second, you taught
her to read the words of your jargons and made her believe they had
    meaning,
so that her intellect became the shadow of your incompetence
and she could share your stare into vacancy.
Mothers of God ! — But when this Man breaks His silence
and speaks that Word which is the Husband of the heart,
and the answer and the direction and the Far Goal,
the spell of your tyranny will be broken
and she and She and SHE
will remember the dawn and the first Adamic walking and companionship.

25

We walk, but we are dead men who walk. We speak to one another
across unbridgeable distances. We dance, but never know our partner.
We sing without ever hearing the notes of our song. We pray
and since all prayer is answered, we spawn a new disease every year.
We beget ourselves in lust and come into the world angry at our own act.
We sleep in fear, and awake in a bluster in order to dispel our fears.
We search the stars for Truth and dig into the earth to find Being —
and the eyes of our souls stare into the darkness of our walled hearts.
We have mocked one another, "Let us be friends and drink together"—
and secretly put poison in each other's glass.
We have been told, perhaps, that God has come into the world again,
and have smiled, "Another escapist !" or "I heard a lunatic speaking."
We chuckle, "We will let off a big bomb.
We will kill our children rather than abdicate our anger."

26
... And the country of Adam — the place
of any one Adam of us, easily expandable
by any man with divine mind, that is, shed of limitation,
a human-being person, to the whole earth. But
when men had turned their backs on the saints and the saint-in-them,
they had to wave-beat it and foot-slog it (or ride on 'orses).
And knowing no longer the gods of God —
thy gods O Man — they employed men
to write prayers for them to mouth
to No-God, that is, after the theologians had decided
'oo exactly 'e was. But, of course
it was Ares the Blusterer whom they worshipped
after changing his name to "Jehovah", which
was a funny way of saying "Jhoah", which is "God" in English.

27
Ares they worshipped; and sacrificed lovely Jesus
on Ares' altar — blood-scarlet for cardinals,
blood-purple for kings — denied Jesus
arisen again as Mohammed and painted
pictures of a man they called Christ minding sheep;
and played shepherd-games — reviving the Roman cult,
paying poets to write verses about it. Thus, Christ-Ares —
supreme muddlement, destruction of all true values in Art and living;
the kings and the general herd of business men and workers
never quite sure *which* one was in their prayers — and the theologians
swopping them round as suited the particular policy of the rulers.
But the Perfect Masters and the saints guarded the lovely Way of God,
guarded Art, and showed it secretly to a few — a little, not much,
having in mind the need of tempering its wind to shorn sheep.

28
Ares they worshipped: hated Jesus the great Ascetic, Opposer
of planned economy and settled way of life,
terrible Slayer of Rome their pilgrimage — cunningly
killed Him again (denied His-Mohammed),
made Him into a Christ
benevolent of their policy of trade expansion; decked Him,
Avatar-warrior of supreme majesty and loveliness,
in cap and bells — supreme insolence:
started first by Paul
opposition of Chargemen Peter — Paul, a Roman at heart,

a soap-box orator who won the day of the church.
But Peter's line was carried down
by lovers of solitude successfully until
Jesus appeared again in Arabia. Similar to the Thirtythree in China.

29
"God made sense to look out." So we looked out
(and up and down — three dimension), and went out
and shouted horizons; and now
whizzing in bubble-whizzing across and up and down
bubble-earth whizzing in bubble-space of nowt.
Saying, "Breakfast in New York, lunch in the Andes in the palace
where the Sun-god kept seven hundred virgins." "The Sage,
sitting where he is, travels everywhere, sees everything, knows everything"—
What was that? That makes someone inside you
jelly-shake, doesn't it? ... Yogi stuff — hypnotism ...
Have a quick one out-of-a-glass or in-bed-with-a-girl —
that'll make you feel better.
Don't forget
we leave in the morning by the Paradise Flight.

30
We moved out. We spread over the ground like locusts.
Population increase brings hunger; we had to eat —
but called it "progress", called it "culture".
But there can be prayer before meat, and thanksgiving after —
and you don't HAVE to kill your host and his wife and kids
or put poison in their water hole. We moved out into the sun
and became shut of the sun. We built cathedrals in New York
(as earlier in Rome) to the god of No-sun.
We designed a Picasso to split the atom of line and colour
to excite our nerves; we compounded an Eliot
to brew an opiate to soften the shock; we invented an Obey
to amuse us by representing on the stage
Avatar Noah as a doddering old man, and a Fry
to whinny and gambol and trot off again with a neigh.

31
And I. Khan said: "In India the idea has always been
towards music of a single instrument, suitable
for a cave, a grass-hut or a temple, and a solo singer.
In the West they like an orchestra that can be heard through a park."

One *would* wonder why a man who wants
to show some devotion to God, to make sounds well-pleasing
to Him, should need a hundred instruments, and perhaps an organ
and two hundred men and women bawling and screaming at one another.
One would suppose that he thought God was a long way off
or had brass ears. One wonders why they want
to play a piano faster and faster — Minute Waltz got down to 51·2 sec.—
And make notes run together to make colours, and try and make them
tell stories, as though there was no more pigments and brushes
or language with lovely words to use.

32
And Master Kung said that a man ought
to spend most of his time studying poetry and music and divine manner
and being very quiet inside himself. And Laotze advised him
"Do it in yourself, Kung, and don't try and *teach* other men.
If you try to be some use in the world
you burden the people with your own insufficiency."
And Jesus pointed out that the usefulness of Solomon's public office
was inferior to the uselessness of flowers.
And Moses had much the same ideas re usefulness
when he said to God, "Don't pick on me as a worker."
And Junaid wouldn't budge neither for Sari nor the other Sheikhs nor
the people's entreaties — the Prophet Himself had to order him.
And also John who wrote lovely verses preferred wandering
around the paddocks or through the olive-groves talking with God.

33
We moved out, footslogging it to receding horizons,
and began bubble-whizzing dreaming of . . .
and Aphrodite making a damn-fool of herself
going to bed with Ares, because Hephaestus threw
strong bands around them
and the other gods witted the joke of it
(even Zeus, probably on aside)
and she was well-wishing to be free of the Blusterer's embrace.
But Athene, virgin-born Virgin, who loved heroes and lovely speech
was forwarding Odysseus on the path of fortune
and feeding the soul of blind Demodocus with lovely Art,
touching his eyes with her wand and giving him
clear seeing and winged words,
pinions to the souls of men desiring news of God.

34

After Mohammed, Art raining over the earth, seas of flowers:
Troubadours, the Friends of God ("Mohammedan" and "Christian");
the Flower and the little flowers of Assisi (calling Him Jesus);
Dante writing love poems to Him (calling Him Beatrice)
but, bad luck, wandering off into a hell and heaven of self-imagining
rather than, as Majnun, following his "Leila" to the grace of His feet.
"Yer certainly know how ter sculpt," said Hui Neng,
"but yer don't know a damned t'ing about Zen."
Mohammed denied; and the false theology of the Son:
soon after this, the line of the saints coming to an end.
After this, men could only get themselves out of the way
occasionally,— only sometimes could Art show her pure form
to men's eyes, and men make purely offerings,
likenesses in *likeness* of the creativity of God.

35

With Dante & Co., the rot set in. Love still there, but delusion
of self-doing creeping in — not lover lost in lineaments of Beloved;
and characterization instead of attributes of God — begun
by Euripides who came after Aeschylus, after Homer the Pure.
The practice of writing is: Mr. Bacon said, to make one an exact man;
(the Pandava brothers' Guru, "Don't shoot until you can *see* the target");
the scholar Coomaraswamy said, to imprison fire against senility.
We define it, a burnt-offering insistent on present altar.
Since Dante & Co. we've been doing it ever since:
seriousness of the immature, craftsmen to each other,
children playing Prophets, "I saw, I saw"—past tense;
"I *feel*"— artists as "antennae of the race":
"No Guru no Shishya", the wrong way round.
Tongues before we were *ears* — sculpture without Zen.

36

Since Dante and Chaucer — a handful of work from Shakespear
(subtracting what he SAID from what he was paid to say);
from Burns, a poesy; from Rimbaud, a sentence
in search of a Master; from Nietzsche and Whitman,
two pages each, one for themselves, one for God;
Blok and Mayakovsky, two voices looking for a piano;
Lorca, a guitar seeking two lips behind a fan of olive trees;
from Synge and O'Casey and James Weldon Johnson, each three flowers,
one for each of the Trinity; from Gabriela Mistral,

five candles lit on the platter of Arti; from **Pound,**
harmony on a lute played with a rifle-trigger,
and sometimes almost making *music*; from Charles Chaplin
a rose growing out of a violin. The rest yoicking words into yawns
and snapping them with damp fingers.

37
Since the lovely Unison-singers — from Palestrina,
some nectarines picked at dawn and eaten in a cathedral
in place of bread which had gone dry; from Vittoria,
a bunch of Muscatel grapes at dusk with the bloom on them;
Dufay and DuPrey, each a choir of young boys; from Monteverdi,
a crystal cup holding a drop of blood turning to wine;
from Purcell, a golden note on a silver plate;
Bach, a shaft of textured light humming Sunward;
from Beethoven, after he had vociferated himself into *some* silence,
fourteen pieces of good old-men's talk; from Mozart,
also good old-men's talk (subtracting what he SAID from what . . .);
from Bellini, three flowers tied with garlic; from Liszt, five lights
for an Arti; from Villa Lobos, an ox-cart singing; from Bartok, sound
of clear water towards morning. The rest swilling sentimental violence.

38
Since the iconography of the Real, and the Manuscripts, and the wood
and stone carving — from Sassetta, a wall and the meeting of two saints;
from Cimabue, a portrait of St. Francis how he might have looked;
a Stupa at Assisi and another at Padua from Giotto;
from Fra Angelico, a voice from a clear sky;
from Memling, a clear sky singing in a woman holding
a tiny Jesus; from Piero della Francesca
a ray of sunlight and viols on the crib of Govinda-Bambino;
from El Greco, hope that believed it was colour;
from Blake, two portraits of Christ, one about Jesus;
from Cezanne and Braque, a few areas of definition to take the place
of sentimental windows; from Juan Gris and Chagall,
a violin and a white pony, each carrying a rider. The rest
mud up to the hocks, painting their eyelids pink and green.

39
Surely a niggardly total: five drops of milk
strained out of five million buckets of blood.
The night. The night. Strong steel and hard concrete —

and our hearts, deserts of spent foam. A Wind — and a rain of fire.
Divine Jesus, divine Jesus, I grieve not for you —
our insolence is only one of the lesser jewels
surrounding the central jewel of your Crucifixion, thou
of God and God, Creator of universes. I grieve
because of you-of-Krishna and the Krishna of you and the Sameness
of your sword and the bow of Rama and the two eyes of the Living One
which have looked at me and the insolence of my still-being.
But, by God, He has made promises — for the fulfilment of which
I will follow Him in each next of His births
and stand silently before Him awaiting the sword's lightning of His Word.

40
Surely a niggardly total: Art dead
if it had not remained living in the hearts of God's saints
elsewhere in rag-bundles by the roadside, in bazaars and jungles —
God's darlings awaiting God's here-arrival of BABA.
Night of our dreaming of four hundred years of piddle-puddling
in pigments and notes and words of attitudinization,
adventuring mightily in far-journeying
and host-conquered — the Holy War not even begun:
the planes of glory untouched by our feet.
BABA ! be thou our turning and surrenderance
and profitable obedience, Thou Axis about Whom
turn universes and our pitiable aspiration.

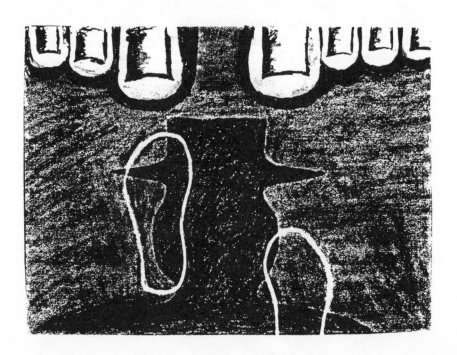

PART II

1

The seasons are slow for men, but swift for God:
drought-drag of flesh-chains on spirit, wings of Zeus' eagle
motionless in the empyrean — illustrated by
the story of the disciple sent to fetch water from the river.
There he met a woman, forgot about water, married her;
acquired much money, acquired children,
lost the lot the lot, and her. Set out again
upon the pilgrim road and came to his Guru's door
freshly suppliant. Twelve years in his time
had passed. "Half an hour is a long time to spend
getting a bucket of water and not bring it back,"
the Guru commented. Drought-drag of flesh-chains;
while above Manasarowar by eternal Kailas
circles the divine Swan without movement in mirror-gazing.

2

Nothing ever happens. Happening is dreaming. For instance,
as Meher Baba said one day during the Sahavas, "Here you are all
sitting in this hall thinking that your being here is real —
but I assure you you are only dreaming it. Say, tonight,
when you go to sleep, you are dreaming that you are sitting here,
and someone comes in in your dream and tells you you are
only dreaming. You will reply,
'I am not dreaming, I am actually experiencing sitting here
listening to Baba's discourse with all the others around me!'
But in the morning you will awake and remember it
as a dream. So I tell you that one day you will really awaken
and know for certain that everything you have done was only a dreaming.
I am the Ancient One — so is each one of you.
But whereas I have awakened, you are still held in your dreams."

3

Mohammed said, "It is incumbent upon every believer to acquire
        knowledge."
How much, and of what? According to Ali b. Uthman al-Jallabi
        al-Hujwiri,
"Sufficient of the world to earn one's living and support a family.
Knowledge is immense and life is short; time
is precious — don't fritter it away picking up bits of

information about this and that, but use it to find Truth."
Anas b. Malik said, "The wise aspire to know, the foolish to relate."
Mohammed said, "The devotee without divinity is like a donkey turning
    a mill."
Hatim al Asamm said, "I have chosen four things to know — the rest
have discarded: that my daily bread is apportioned to me,
so I don't strive to augment it; that I owe God a debt
which no one else can pay; that one (Death) pursues me,
and I have prepared myself against the day when he catches up with me;
that God is observing me, and I am ashamed to do what I ought not."

4
Sufficient knowledge of the world to earn a living and
to buy three books: the Bible (at this time it is called "God Speaks"),
a book of the lives of saints, a book of living verse; to buy
a musical instrument and the price of some lessons from a master of it.
Sufficient knowledge of who and what one is
in order to live as a human-being admidst people,
in order not to be wholly a user and a hypocrite; in order
to begin to long for "other" than what one is, i.e. Self or God.
Sufficient knowledge of the states of God (see "God Speaks")
in order to appreciate the absolute necessity of a Master,
and enough wit to find Him and enough gumption
to obey Him implicitly once one has found Him.
All extra knowledges are "toggles before your ass's nose"
to keep you plodding up the never-ending dusty road:

5
So that Aphrodite-of-one shall not go on for the rest of one's life
making a damn fool of herself bed-romping with Ares the Blusterer.
But divine Jesus was tougher than Mohammed and His commentators,
or than Master Kung, and said
that there is only one thing you need know and that is,
"I am the way, and yer haven't got Buckley's chance of gettin' t' God
except through Me. So you'd better leave yer poor old
mother and father and kid sister and yer oil and steel empires
an' tag along and, as Khizr said to Moses,
Don't ask no fool questions of Me because I'm a busy man,
but just be handy in case I get the WHIM
to give you a whack over the head and let some Daylight
into your thick skull (stone head), or in My utter kindness
plunge you into terrible remorse as I did My beloved Peter."

6

Books. Books. A weariness to the flesh, as Solomon said. Dead meat
riddled with maggots by the time they're off the press. And unless
one has the transforming breath of a Jesus — but then
one don't need them. "Excellent guides until you find the Way,"
said Abu Sa'id after he had buried his. A book is a book
when it contains the Name of God. "There have been
84,000 Prophets and each one left a Book and each Book
contained one word — God," said Abu'l Fadl to the young seeker.
"God Speaks" is a Book of a book, the Book of this age
written by God "to appease
the intellectual convulsions of the mind of men."
For as its Author states, "to *understand* the infinite, eternal Reality
is NOT THE GOAL of individualized beings in the Illusion of Creation . . .
Reality . . . is to be *realized* by conscious experience."

7

"God Speaks" is also the first time
God has used the English language to tell us something
He wanted to tell us. Almost like He had
got tired of Sanskrit or Greek or Arabic or Hebrew
and had the idea He would learn a new language,
the lingo of the majority of the most dumb of the most, most
gross-conscious of human-beings that ever were
upon the face of the earth, who have forgotten about Him
the most longest and most consistently; and
who never remember what they read because
as Coomaraswamy, A.K. pointed out, the spread of literacy
is the decline of culture. We can all read,
but what do we read ? Someone's killed someone, or would like to;
someone's seen something which we haven't and thinks we should know:

8

someone's invented a new gadget
          or a new form of budget
          or a different smelling soap
          or a new cereal
          or the improved scope
          of a radio aerial
          or the odds of 'orses
          or some social behaviour courses or
the other various kinds of anusial belching

that keeps our feet squelching in veil of mud
across heart-word and response
and the soul
dancing a jig or a rock 'n' roll
nuzzling a carrot
suspended from the point of a bayonet.

9
English, a developed language. Milton, we are told,
made it resonate — but why did he have to stand on his head to do it?
Milton blind; and Homer all-seeing. No one seems to 'ave mentioned
that resonance is a quality of the heart. When Vivekananda
got up in Chicago and merely pronounced the word "Brothers!"
half the assembly got up on their hind legs and cheered. Vivek
knew the "blank-paper scriptures" by heart — in fact
his heart was painted with whiteness.
His heart encompassed brotherhood — brother was he
in true sonship of his Guru — so when
the particular of this general light-condition
occurred on his tongue and he said "Brothers!" the resonance
reverberated in the souls of his audience — and their souls
remembered their natural posture of verticality and they stood up.

10
No doubt, as Sankaracharya pointed out, "all songs are to Brahman"
     (God),
so, it could be asserted that all expression is Art. But
some songs are the long way round — the round of the rounds
of a few million (perhaps) more births, and some
are a flight direct to the heart of God; just as all men
are drunk — some with the world, some with love for God;
which is just the difference between your caged crooner and
mud-painter and violent-poet and a Mirabai or Sappho or Chatti Baba.
Guernica is parochial; Siva-Bhairav at Kailas, universal.
Guernica, the rage of a man against conditions imposed by *others;*
Kailas, the destruction of self-imposed obstacles to Self.
Guernica, an expression of barbarism destroying itself;
Kailas, the expression of civilization continually renewing itself.
Guernica is reflection; Kailas is a statement.

11

Art is an act of love — an imperishable statement
cut in stone, uttered in tones and words or through the movements
of the dancer,— and thus impressioned in the "material" of mind,
continually contemporary and continuously accessible to one who loves:
as act, self-sufficient — useless
for thy works of progress, O man; as statement,
revealment of the beauty of God, and proof of His eternal Existence.
When David or Tukaram danced before God, a harmony of movement
        was
impressed on the minds of people who didn't even see the dance;
when Solomon or Namdev sang, music was entering into people's lives;
when Enoch walked with God, walking was again beautiful;
when the "Friends of God" talked with Him, speech became lovely;
when Mohammed offered His "5 prayers", the
the hearts of men listened and inclined toward prayer.

12

The sun is everyday renewing the world of nature and men.
Even though you shut yourself in a room, sun is in the food you eat
and in the fire, or radiator by which you try to melt your bones.
Avatar is everyday renewing men's hearts even though they encase 'em
in concrete and steel. If anyone denied the existence of the sun
he would be thought crazy — yet denial
of the One who sustains the heart (motivator of thought
and organ of insight) is considered normal and scientific.
Science which rejects reasoning is divorced from Science;
art which takes no account of intuition has become separated from Art.
Come ! an end to equivocation and mud-puddling
and accepting the advice of Canute's counsellors —
you have not yet harnessed the ocean or God's Breath;
not even yet measured the "spots" on the physical sun.

13

And on one hand you have Ezra Pound with knowledge of many languages
confused and disappointed because
all of truth cannot be contained in any one language,
and on the other, Bullah Shah with the powers of God
arising out of mastery of a single letter. On one hand
Basudev confusing the issue with learned commentary
and on the other divine Chaitanya, scholar also, *using* the texts
as a runway to take his listeners towards Truth.
Words, words — but the Name of God

given to the eager and pure disciple by the precious **Guru**
is the key which unlocks the doors of words
shut fast on the printed page.
The Name is the living breath of Truth which blows
whereso It will and can unlock even the doors of hearts.

14
Because, Mr. Pound, you don't need ten languages to say it.
Any *one* Babel-tongue will do so long
as one has thoroughly learned the word "turning",
and has turned (repented) and is facing in the direction,
and has said, Give me a word by which I may know words.
Ah (ha)! this is the very and entirely bones and soul of the matter
of poetry — the turning and unlearning and returning;
and the mind cheerful and high-hoped and open
dwelling upon the heart's tone which is the Voice of the Word
in a man — which was how Valmiki received the Ramayana;
and Homer said, "Tell me, O Virgin of God, thou pure Brightness,
tell me the words of my speaking — for of ourselves
we hear only rumours and know nothing." And thus
every poet who is an answer to his own prayer.

15
And Tukaram, *after* he was schooled in daily conversation
with Krishna, starts writing verses at Krishna's behest (for God
loves poets who can rightly sing His praises). A poet
is a swift arrow of light in the darkness at fat necks supporting
pin-headed thinking ("unless your neck becomes
as thin as a hair"); an idle, glorious one,
bane of progress of production-lines and bitumen
boiled with the sweat of breath which should be savoured sacrifice
to God. I labour my point. Certainly. Labours
are little hammers — and hammers, hand or "jack",
is the only way of breaking stone — not that Baba won't do it
with a single Word — but, if we had already lost our ears
in fine poetry and our eyes in love-glancing,
we would have *some* accommodation for Baba's Word of breaking.

16
But this is not a denial of learning.
A man of learning *and* whose heart is open
can bring others to his own station, whereas

a man of heart alone enjoys sight of God but helps no one.
But a man with learning, the gate of whose heart is shut
so that God has not come into it and reshapen it
and well-pleased taken His seat there and receives the man's love,
a man in whom the vivifying breath of a Jesus or Tilopa has not moved,
is a designer in wind-blown sand,
a winnower of straw-chaff.
He calls that which is passing, real, and asserts
that the Real is false — a destroyer
of culture and a betrayer of lovely Art,
a bubble-mouth man, bubble slobber
of hail on the green shoots of young intellect.

17
On the one hand, the man unspeakably glorious;
and on the other, the woman unnamably beautiful.—
"Sometimes," a disciple said, "when I repeat the Name
I feel the qualities of the moon — I become
the moon and experience bliss.
Sometimes when I repeat the Name
I feel the qualities of the sun — I become
the sun, and overpowered, fall senseless to the ground."
Moon-gleam and sun-beat —
Artemis' gentle arrows and the rivers and words of enchantment,—
the Sun-god's brazen arrows wounding
the mouth of the parched earth, and it still calling.—
How long is the path to God's feet ? —
Rain, rain, the healing of gentle rain.

18
A "human" being — a divine man ! taking
"Hu" as "of God" and deriving man from "manas", mind.
A human being — that final vehicle
which Spirit moulded with care and loving eagerness
and informed. Which the angels
were commanded by God to worship, but which Iblis hated
and ever since have the Devil's descendants
hated it and conditioned it and twisted it to serve their purposes.
A human being — laboured towards
through the endless ages of evolution, a man and a woman,
blue-printed in Paradise (Eden), fitted together precisely

and realized in actuality after the Exile and immeasurable wandering
in the perfect saints; but perfected completely
in the Men-God, the Perfect Masters and in the God-Man, Avatar.

19
"A human-bein'— that's an interestin' word. It's got to do
with a man actin' somethin' like God. Some don't.
Must be somethin' to do with evolution. People
don't get rid of it all. That's why
yer get some actin' as mean as a snake or as cunnin'
as a dingo or as randy as a bull.
I knew a man once couldn't look at any woman
without wantin' to go at 'er.
But I saw one woman handle 'im. Just looked at 'im
and 'e changed colour and gave a kind of a snort
like a bull wot was suffocatin', and made off. I said to her,
'That's a pretty powerful sort of a look, Miss.' 'Yes,'
she says, 'I call it my mirror look. They get
their horns tangled up in it and don't like wot they look like.' "

20
As with most popular notions, the notion that travel is broadening,
the reverse is true — because
it ties ever more tightly the knots in the net of the senses;
it causes one to see many things and remember few;
to make many acquaintances and few friends: it leads the imagination
on to tomorrow and prevents mind dwelling on the moment of today;
it scatters affection and prevents love from manifesting;
it makes meditation difficult and prayer impossible.
The ideal man is one who has never been beyond the boundaries
of his own district; who, except that he must eat, or to visit his friend,
hardly leaves his house; who welcomes the world as a visitor,
and after a little while conducts it courteously to the door.
The Very Ideal Man is a Bullah Shah — unlettered save for one letter,
unminded save for one Object before his mind's eye.

21
And the "problem of children" because we have despised
the saints and ridiculed the ways of Art and heeded not
the successive Word of Brightness. When
words no longer have value,
when a man's word is given lightly

and love is barter and art dressed in whoredom and mocked
and the eye does not look straightly
and the mouth drops filth
and convulses before the gentle word "brother" and
the ear is denied solitary listening and is sold
into whoredom for lust of advertising and propaganda,
the children have no one to whom they can turn,
no one whom they can trust: secureless,
homeless and parentless and wandering they become.

22
And it is that the undisciplined parent, the parent
who loves not pupilship, says to the child, "Don't!" And in the word
    "don't"
the child hears, "Continue in what you are doing." Because
in the undisciplined parent's word is the injunction to ignore it.
And it is that the undisciplined government comprising men who love not
learning and have not acquainted themselves with the Divine Truths,
nor sought to model themselves in the image of Art, it is, that when
they make a law, contained in that law is the command to break it.
And it is that because of these things this age is an Avataric Age —
a time when we, Man, have sunk to a low level of living and being,
when the limit of the violation of the divine in man and the human of God
has been reached; and only by the fully and perfect Descent of Himself
as a man can He re-establish the Way of Virtue,
the Way of pupilship and love and delight of human-ness in men.

23
Little streams run towards big streams, and the rivers loose themselves
into the ocean; but the streamlets of God, the little children,
have no one to bear them to the divine Ocean of their origin —
they spill over on bitumen and concrete in small escaped floods.
Ghost-talk in school rooms — male voice, female voice, talking ghost-talk.
What will we tell the little children? Tell them about animals
that frisk on the earth. There are pictures of them in the picture books,
ghost pictures. Little lamb, little lamb — lamb chops for breakfast, too!
Outside sun in the sky. Get up teacher, and organize some games —
they have forgotten play-way — you must show them how.
Bring them inside again. Let the lady-voice and the gentleman-voice
tell them about Red Indians or Aborigines. No stories
of King Arthur or King Rama and valour and gentleness and courtesy;
no poems of desperate lovers; no Little Preludes of John Sebastian Bach.

24

"Jesus! If only someone would make some nice music.—
Music oughta start somewhere within a man's heart, and come out
and *surprise* 'im with a sort uv delight — like rain
after a long dry spell, or like a bloody lovely moon
coming up outa the ocean. It oughta make a man
feel like shoutin' like those chaps did
when the mornin' stars sang together. Morning stars! —That's
poetry. Jesus — if only some chap would write a bit of poetry
or some music which would sound like that — so that
the Living Christ Himself would nod 'is 'ead in approval!
Jesus — I bet even the bloody cows would dance and the bloody dingoes
nibble grass alongside the sheep. Even men might stop cuttin'
little lambs' throats and eatin' them — if only someone
made some real good music, music as lovely as God."

25

Christ of a calculation for a scientist! that
purely by mathematics he adjudged this an Avataric Period
and that Lord Baba had again come into the world
and the exact place where He could be found.
Christ of a theme for a fugue in twelve parts — the disciples
and their heavenly course around Him,
their service and adoration. But it seems
that shepherds once had more ñous than intellectuals have now.
The world is a vaudeville-show: item:
Demonstration of the exact effect of radiation on human tissue.
Item: Demonstration of how exactly a satellite world
will be able to control the earth. Item: Demonstration
of the reaction of a monkey's nerves to our most recent music.
The next Item will be a little song-number by Avatar.

26

Ideograms: draw a circle = All = also Sun = concentration
of Divine Light (pull yourself together, old man) = Avatar who shines
equally on saint and sinner, and from Whom came the sun and stars
and air and fire and water and the lovely earth — Life of all things
in the earth, and of men and women the Awakener. The lovely One.
Draw five lines coming out of the circle, one up, one each side, two down
and you have a man, evolution's end and possibility of Self-knowing. Draw
lines radially = wheel = bondage in rebirth. Sun beside wheel = man
found by a Perfect Master = involution = taking the Path back to God.

116

Draw a pot — any sort of pot = any sort of man or woman with heart.
Put two wheels to it = heart moving in balance.
A well-wrought vase instead of any old pot = a mature man or woman.
Attach wings to it = a saint; wings and a spout = flying and pouring =
a perfect saint, one who is with God *and* helps people.

27

Men of God (artists) and defenders of lovely Art: Paul, the real Paul
in Jesus' footsteps, first to deny the world and flee to the desert,
but when Anthony visited him after sixty or seventy years
inquired compassionately —"Are men still building cities?"
Paul, for whose body lions dug the grave. And Bemus the gentle,
whom the desert beasts frisked around when he walked abroad at night,
and he would draw water from a well and give them cups of it. And Theon,
who kept silence for thirty years, and in whose eyes an angel stood.
And Hrut, who when a child mocked him, called the child to him
and gave him a gold ring and kind advice, so that the child said,
"Thy manliness I will bear in mind all my life."
And Kari the sudden, who never thought twice about dealing a blow,
even in a strange Earl's house and all the Earl's battle-men at table;
and trusted his life to the manhood of his enemy Flosi.

28

And Macarius, who was a lover beyond all others, to whom
God returned the grapes after their going the entire round of the desert.
And Hyperichus, who said, "Better to eat flesh and drink wine
than eat your brother's flesh by back-biting." And Achilles,
"If thou wouldst sup broth, go down into Egypt." And Milarepa,
"If you want condiments, put in a few more nettles."
And Paphnutius, to whom God showed his equal in a street singer who
had been a robber and who at Paphnutius' word threw away his pipes
and used his skill in music to bring his mind and heart into harmony.
And Isidore, at peace with his wife and an angel guiding the team
while he conversed with God. And Flosi whose rotten ship
was "sea-worthy enough for an old man ready to die."
And Njal, lawman and man of love, who slew none but accepted his own
    slaying
And Bergthora his wife, who met death bravely with him.

29

Light. Light. Lu subdued the floods; Rama threw a bridge across them;
Noah outroad them. Light. Light. Light on grass and leaf,
petal-light of pink and white in the spring,
fruit-light of early summer and summer, snow-light

about the feet of Tai Shan or Meru;
Moses' woollen shirt (according to Al Junaid);
Telemachus' woollen shirt; Milarepa's
shirt of woven angel's breath. Light — flood of the mind,
and dress of the soul,— the movement of which in a man
through his hands or speech is called Art.—
The Golden Age (time of the reign of Virtue) is in perpetuity,
as Bhanudas showed the false-worshipping king in respect to Pandharpur;
and Paradise is merely the passing landscape
of nothingness in the mirrors of the Perfect Masters.

30

Unless a man takes his stand *against* the world of a dying civilization,
unless he stops discriminating the patterns of shadow
and turns his face to the Sun of the Living God, he shall
in nowise grow his life into a harvest against his old age and for others;
he shall in nowise become a singer of lovely song,
a devotee praiser of Avatar's deeds; nor shall Sophia
with bangled arms and smiling sweetly come to him
and kiss his mouth into awakening. Unless a man
sits down and stops fattening his guts (guts, a convenient symbol

of the gross plane) he shall in nowise avoid ruinous belly-fat poverty;
unless a man sits down and determines the tone and colour of his heart
he shall never be able to obey the seasons nor himself.
Unless . . . and takes thought within his heart he shall in nowise
increase his stature and again become a little child.

31

Shave your head, and pour dust upon it and wait
until He calls, for any other mirror but Him will deceive you
and keep your ass plodding up the dusty road. Sit down
like a plant and wait His sun, for all other suns rise only to set.
The lover waits for the night, for only then does beauty become visible
and his ardour is decorated with kisses. To him
day is night because its light leads into darkness; whereas
night is day because therein shines his true love.
It is because the lover is immature that the Beloved
draws a veil of beauty over the face of His truth —
it is because of this veil that anguished idleness begins.
But when the lover sees Leila's face in the roadside dust
the Beloved weeps one tear in which the lover is drowned,
smiles one smile which becomes the lover's illumination.

32

Once men burnt the flesh of their flesh upon altars —
and God was savour or not of the sacrifice. And the Rain fell
or didn't, and the remaining flesh was lit, or remained opaque,
and the devotee took the sun-path to immortal Self, or the moon-path
to another birth. Wrought their lives in likeness
of God's creativeness; told stories in stone and words
of Avatar's lives — His acts of compassion and loveliness, so that
wherever people looked they saw images of God.
Then men started telling stories about men, and
characterization and situation took the place
of the attributes and deeds of God: the fields of light,
the battle-fields of the soul (Kurukshetra), became
the wars of men fought for some woman or a strip of earth.—
O Helen thou lovely one hiding Truth in your bright curls!

33

Worshippers of Ares we became: ring-barkers of forest-silences
of Buddha; obliteraters of the pilgrim-route of Jesus;
defiling the lovely head of God in the dust — Dante
even confining His Friends and Prophets in his own mind-hell.
By God, you would think any fool would know
that the "characters" in the Old Testament and Iliad
were the heroes-of-God overcoming the forces on the planes-of-Him
intent on love and glorious sacrifice, and the Path-conquerors.
But we had been listening to Paul without angel's tongue,
railer and tinkling tympanist surrounding
the lovely theme of Jesus with arpeggios of disorder; we had
imported works of decadent Greeks and paunchy Romans;
and invented "literature", and harnessed our space-poets of Science
into making kitchen-gadgets and guns and exploiting petroleum potential.

34

Brought our divine mind down from azure flight,
kicked out the saint-in-us and banished the saints
to Arabia and Persia and Japan and India and began
wave-beating and foot-slogging over the face of the earth
with our backsides up and our noses along the ground
trying to pick up the musk scent of Truth of our own navel;
and began bubble-whizzing — breakfast in Paris, lunch in Greenland,
dinner and dancing on the terrace under the Northern Lights.
Temples to Ares in New York and Moscow; dress and art fashions

from Paris; a new Pantheon of gods and goddesses
in a place called Hollywood; Elgar in England, and the Church
saving souls of brothel-inmates and taking rent from them; U.S.A.,
big-brother-aid to the whole world, using a thousand steel helmeted
troops to subdue a township and coming second in satellite race.

35

And the Five Perfect Masters quietly cognizing the world
of gangrenous limbs and squint-eyedness, walled city-world overlooking
spent foam desert of accomplishment, and saying among themselves,
It is time to bring him down again, He the Avatar of God
for another spell of world-truing and course-setting,
and because His lovers cannot much longer
breathe with any degree of comfort.— So they
brought Him who was called Manu and Noah and Zarathustra
and Siva and Rama and Krishna and Buddha and Jesus and Mohammed
down, and gave Him birth and watched over Him
with their mother-tenderness and their father-solicitude and brought Him,
the Ancient One and the newest One, again to His God-Man-ness
and handed over to Him the Seal and the Key.
And themselves returned to the Ineffable Mountain of Retirement.

36

And He knew those who were to be His disciples
and He called them to Him in love and service, in gentleness
and warriorship for that War which men ape in their little wars
and took them out on the roads, breathing His own lovely Name
on the breath of their utterance with each step, wiping away
from their faces, with His mother-hand, the sweat and dust of the world,
and as father exampling them and inuring them
to the trials and hardships of manhood. And set out with them
to the haunts of His lovers, the masts and saints,
in jungles and mountain fastnesses and by roadsides and in cities,
and embraced them and fed them and sent them on the next stage
of their journey; and fed the poor and bowed His head down
to their feet — Himself being the poorest among them —
and even visited the West where live the most poor of His poor.

37

And allowed His body to be broken, and the pain of the world
to be centered in His pain. And has done no miracles
except the miracle of love: raised no dead,

but urged us to die to ourselves; given no sight
to the blind, but helped us become blind to illusion:
"I tell you on my divine Authority that they belittle Jesus
who attribute His greatness to mere miracles which any fourth-planer
still wrapped in illusion himself can perform."
Manifested unlimitedness in limitation; established
divinity in the midst of barbarism; brought lovely Art,
love's pure act, again upon earth; raised
once again the Banner ablaze with gathered Brightness
of "Love God"— that men again shall joy in the works of their hands,
and in love, and remember that they are the sons of God, and God.

38
Thus ... and thus it will ever be — the One, as Jesus,
raising again the Banner of Moses draggled in the wind;
and those who really loved Moses fled to His feet as Jesus
and folded their hands before Him and cast down their hearts
before His again-Brightness. And the One, as Mohammed,
raising again the Banner of Jesus bleached by wilful interpretation;
and those who loved Jesus with somewhat of the love
with which He should be loved flocked to Him exalting in God's
mercy and towardness. And the One, as Baba,— and those
who are of the Law and the Love and the Humanity
are dancing with new joy, and casting themselves in surrenderance
and measured abandon into His fire of melting and remoulding
nearer to soul's vision of true heart-shape. Thus it will ever be —
the cry of the Dawn, and the weeping before the Risen Sun.

39
Because you are love, which is Existence
                    which is Knowledge
                    which is Bliss
you always gave out the Heart Doctrine, Love Me, love Me.
But you have found it necessary also to take up swords and whips.
You have accepted thorns and arrows and crucifixions,
but you have rolled many heads in the dust
and stripped many of their all except God.
Therefore are you known by some as the Lamb and by others as the Lion.
To some you are Fullness and to some Emptiness,
to some the Treasure-keeper and Bestower,
to some the only Poor-one and great Beggar —
you beg a morsel of our love
O God, and you give us our divine Self.

40

Art is an act of love — the SHOCK, whereby the soul
awakens to awareness of itself; and understands
that the world is the shadow of the Real,
that "everything is passing except His Face";
and that all experience has but one purpose and end,
to cause one to renounce the world as an empty dream.
Art is an act of love — the cry of the devotee as a sword
in his heart cutting an accommodation in which
the Sun of majesty and loveliness may rise;
and the furnace of tears,
and the smokeless fire of secret sighs, and the blood
turning to milk, and death in eternal Existence.
Art is the loveliness of God embodied in a Man —
God as that Man in His lovely acts to men.

PART III

1

Return, O Man, O brother and sister of me, return
O myself, before the tide turns at His Speaking
and we are carried by His-Noah's flood whitherward like fools
drunk in an open boat on the ocean, to the Way of Art and God.
Stay with God. For He is not only the All-Mighty Creator,
but our Brother and Friend. His counsel is better
than the wit of men, for He is Deathless and men are born to die.
He is Knowledge and Existence, and knows all the paths to Him
and leads those by the short path who surrender their path to Him.
He stirs up and urges forward, He retards and holds back
till the right time. He drives one on to glorious victory,
He hurls another into defeat — Andromache
shall not receive of thee Hector Pelides' glorious arms
for this would be to rob Thetis of victory whom God had promised.

2

Art is a statement in praise — His *craft* in us
fashioning us in *likeness* of Himself: the Perfect Masters,
His consummate works; the saints, nearing completion;
us, His beginnings. He is the only singer: He sings
the creation; and His singing supports and destroys it. As Poet
He gives us Scriptures for our guidance; in the saints He sings
His own praises and dances because He loves dance. He builds
cathedrals and temples and mosques, carving their columns
in exact variety, cuts and paints figures of Himself
on their walls for His love of proportion and as text-books
for us of right living. His is the only "iconography of the Real":
that of ourselves that we do is from the laboured breathing
of *un*seeing, *un*hearing and divisional thinking — dreamers
depicting in dream a monstrous confusion of dreaming.

3

A tree is a tree. It is not creative, but reproductive.
A man is a man and likewise creates nothing.
The image is already in the stone, the bridge
in steel, awaiting revealment and spanning
at the word of God in a man's hand.
Mind, which prompts us, "we are the doer", is a mirror-house

of distorting in which Self is deluded by being imaged
as everything other than Self. A man
as a man can cease from foolishness and begin to love —
begin to repeat the Name of God in his heart,
seek in his heart the Beloved's lovely face,
wait patiently for a word or a note or some intimation
of His form and make his many notes and words and outlines
pleasing to Love's ears and eyes. Only one become One may create.

4

The only reason for reviving painful experiences
is to mature one's outlook, not feed excitement in others,
sowing in them the seed of future pain, excusing it
as legitimate communication. "And he who was to become
the Buddha, the inspirer of his time, the Rest and Spring of men
for the next 500 years", was sheltered from pain
until his mature mind could grasp it and subdue it.
Being dragged through hell by the heels or dreaming
in wan dream a star in lieu of a ripening breast
("I'd liefer ha' a kiss on the mo'," she said), sprawling a nude
across a canvas in rebellion or peopling dead woods with faded
musk of dryad, are neither material nor impetus for art.—"Where
is the Brahmin who taught me?" What splinters of Brahma
by the grace of the True Teacher might have informed them!

5

God made sense turn outward: therefore
man looks out. Now and again a daring man
looks back and finds himself. Now and again
after becoming God he speaks. This *speaking*
is the first art. Often on the homeward track
as the divine Image becomes clear in outline and volume
he sings Its praises. This is the second art —
the lover's drowning in the sweetness of Love's smile.
A Jesus, the Way; an Ali, a door:
now and again a man sees, by God's grace,
God in another man and dares surrender himself to him —
becomes clay in the Master's hands to be moulded
into truly human form, or canvas for a new portrait
truthful in line, exact in volume and lovely in content.

6

The Art of God and His finished works — the *living men:*
Wamadeva said: My glory is like the mountain-tops.
Laotze said: How I glory on the breast of my Mother.
Hui Neng said: You read it to me; I'll tell you what it means.
Ibn 'Arabi said: My heart is a pasture for gazelles and a convent for
     monks.
Shri Hamsa said: I am an instrument played on by the Divine Hand.
Inayat Khan said: Everywhere I look I see Thy winning face.
Francis said: Brother Sun ! — And he wasn't poetizing.
One said: Every day a new heaven is under my feet.
One said: Two that are your masters are my slaves.
One said: Circumambulate me and your pilgrimage is finished.
Attar said: The road was but Myself towards Myself.
Above these, alone in Self-perfected glory and who alone
directly comes down, is God's Avatar.

7

Our works are but a crying toward these Men —
a cry from bondage to their pure release,
a movement in the dark towards their light
like leaves and twigs and branches in the night
moved by the wind and dreaming of the sun;
a turning,— once, when we knew singing,
in delight, spontaneously as flowers to the sky
making our world around us glad with song;
now with remorse and tearings and reaching back
to that which holds us, like roots of grass
uptorn with a chisel-plough clinging to earth,
like drinkers drunk still clinging to the glass, or merely
petulant as children called at meal-time still wanting play;
excursioners returning weary, wanting more.

8

The Word also is food. Therefore the real artists
meditated on the word entrusted them by their teacher
and disciplined their seeing to His form, till their eyes
brightened with tears and praise escaped them.
Then at His command they in their turn spoke to the people
in words or notes or line or chiselled plane
and the people were astonished — and being thus fed,

fed, in their turn, with the word of their work, the earth.
And the breath of God, through the Masters and saints,
brought the rains and the sun in due season.
And when floods came or drought,
they did not huddle in fear or curse the sky,
but looked into their hearts to find the sin
and adjusted their sacrifice to the laws of Nature and God.

9

Without a word of the Word in one's heart,
without a reflection of His light, Whose seventh shadow
is the physical sun, in one's eyes — that is, without
the sacrifice having been made which is savour to God —
no food nourishes, but is poison which paralyses
and finally kills us to our essential Self. With bricks
of dead tissue do we build our vast hospitals,
with the steel of maimed minds do we forge the knife
which performs the operation. The world of nature,
helpless from our helplessness, weeps.
And from her overmuch tears roll the floods
and from her shame and burning shines the sun of drought.
Weeping and burning is nature because of our heedlessness;
and the Winds, finding no home, return to God.

10

So the artist, if he is to sing or write or paint
or play in truth, in praise of love, may not himself, but first
find the golden Thread by which he moves, the lovely Note
from which he has continuous becoming. Then find the Holder of the
        thread,
the lovely Singer, and offer Him his body, speech and mind
in service, nor asking in return the gift of art or anything,
for even this finding and surrenderance is by Grace — Grace
which puts us under eternal obligation of repayment.
Heaven and earth move by the Word alone;
and It moves out from Silence. The Mover
is the Perfect Master, Who holds the thread which binds
each one together in one gathered piece of movement;
Who sings the Song which is our sighs and tears,
our well directed thought and sudden laughter.

11
Once, we knew the lovely form and voice of Art
and trained our children to read its messages
cut in wind and fire and earth and sculpted in fulness
in the human form. Taught them the true sacrifice, "Thou".
Taught them the times of sowing grain in the earth,
grain in the heart and their proper tendance. Taught
them the facts of irrigation of body, mind and earth.
Taught them the true scales and modes. Taught them
the Name of God — that Name in us which made our songs, which
danced before His altars in our hearts and guided our hands
in cutting His memorials. But even then at times
the blood, carrier of light, darkened and we lost our way.
Then we prayed and offered the first born of our loves. And He came
with His shining love again and retrued our vision and retaught His
     Name.

12
So to Mohammed's time — a journey continuous from us to God
and direct from God to us — and for a thousand years after,
when the twilight of our present night set in
and we no longer worked and loved with our eyes upon the Image
in our hearts. We looked out and stared at the horizon
blank with promise of release from our restricted forms.
We looked out — and set out to nowhither
with oars creaking in rowlock and flag hoisted beyond sail at masthead,
wave-beating the waves that beat upon our ships,
scurvy and lice-ridden, our beards and eyes wet
with salt of strange seas and our weeping — not for yellow gold
and fine silks and new foods to glut our glutting, but for a new god
to enthrone above God: one greater than Jesus and Mohammed —
who would not require of us sacrifice and prayer.

13
And we easily found him since he was also
looking for us: in fact he had accompanied us
in our laborious ships and appeared on the land before us
when we landed and greeted us and initiated us into service.
His name was Ares and his bedfellow, Aphrodite.
And they showed us the new altar-building and its rites —

but our seamen, thick-muscled fools of the oar,
still clung to Jesus and we would sometimes come upon them
secretly remembering Him. So we slew Jesus on Ares' altar
and told the men he had died, but that his Spirit
would be upon them if they yielded us good service. Christ-Ares,
two — but in reality, one; and Aphrodite's city
to sack for our pleasure. And to please our men
we wrote them a Book with tunes in it they could easily sing.

14
But because the Word of God may not be denied —
the words of His Word: "Love One God and thy neighbour,"
"think, speak and act truthfully," and "have compassion on all things"—
not only did lovely Art become lost to us — lost
along symphonic horizons and among boudoir pianos and mulish metrics—
but Nature herself, ever loving and dutiful to God
and weeping for His dear Son pierced by arrows and thorns
and bruised by stones, revolted: assumed
new forms of terrible disease; rained floods, burnt the lands
with drought; gave earth's choicest soils back to the oceans
and poisoned the last drops of the divine springs of human affection —
so that the tender word now only growls in our throats, and love's glance
freezes in our eyes or bulges belligerency, and our no-parents-children
sweep the pavements with their eyelashes looking for God.

15
With Renaissance we denied the saint of us, left the House of Love
and marched out, offending the earth with our shod-feet and trumpets,
and settled in foreign lands and occupied ourselves feeding the swine
of appetite; broke ourselves off from the tree of knowledge
and planted the branch in sour soil where it withered and died;
peeled ourselves off from the stem of sweet nourishment
and found it trash in our hand. We made instruments
of dissection and measurement to examine our condition
and ask of the stars; built ships and planes and journeyed
round the earth and into the skies and asked them — and drooled
our non-finding in "poetry" and "music" and painted our wretchedness
into portraits of caricature; turned our universities
(universe-cities) into distribution centres of work-tickets;
and sent armies back to our Parent House to loot its treasury.

16

And our elder brothers looked up from their work and greeted us,
and found themselves facing relentless steel and red fire.
And we opened the doors to the first room of their treasury
which contained the coins of Manual Energy.
And the fire of our eyes blazed and entered into the coin
and we loaded it into our ships and brought it home,
little knowing that it was impregnated with fire,
that it was a Medea's bridal gift of burning.
But it was a burning without smoke and flame,
a secret burning which inflamed our desolation,
fed riot in the blood, consumed our nerve-ends
and smouldered our bones. But we were not knowing this
as we were busy smelting an Image of a new god,
son of Ares, of unlimited power, called Nuclear Fission.

17

In the meantime, back home in the house they had built
according to the plans and specifications laid down
by their Father, the natives were continuing their tribal ways
of song and dance and instructing their children
in the arts of seeing, understanding and memory; tempering
the intellect of their youth so that it could not
be affected by fire, establishing in their breath
the living word and enthroning in their hearts the True God.
Then the Father chose three sons so trained
and sent them to us with weapons of love to take up the war
we had started. And their names were Vivekananda, Coomaraswamy
and Inayat Khan. And the sword of the first made music
like the deep notes of a 'cello and of the second like a fugal
violin and the third, the haunting tones of a primitive flute.

18

Contemptible "History": narrative of wars and earth-betrayals.
Iron-shod feet on earth's breast, steel in her entrails,
fire of the hearth, gift of Prometheus, burning, burning.
Never a chapter or line on the tempered steel of the Planesmen's intellects
and the fire in their hearts melting the bones of limitation;
no accounts of terrible Ocean-crossings storm-whipped
and calm-bound and rhapsodies of further-Shore arrivings —
theme of Iliad, Ramayana and all true books of history.
No histories in text-books for children of Kailas and Mecca

pilgrimages, of building of Borobadur,
of Greek and Ellura stone-cutting *for love,* alone for love;
no Lives of King Janaka and Prince Milarepa, Prince Chaitanya
and forsaken Princess Mira; no *development* of devotion
from Krishna's flute-playing and Siva's making the first vina.

19

Contemptible history — Jesus its date-line and denial
of His frequent and each time perfect Descents. He
is the Unsubtractable, the Unadditional — only a shout and a shock
or a whisper of stirring, a candle or a sun, a little clearance-of-
my-direction or a divine beloved in whom I become annihilate,
to individual men. Contemptible history which teaches
"evolution of consciousness" and "growth of religion". Never
was a time since He unrolled His illusion of universes
— which is now — and Himself pierced the illusion, when men
did not know Him, *become* His Brightness and Art
and themselves pour out His unending song over the earth.
And He raised Five to equalness with Him in His Godhood
and set He-Himself-Them to watch over men and when need
call Him-His-Avatar down for their awakening and direction.

20

At one time He was called Jesus, at another Mohammed,
at one time Krishna, at another Buddha:
each time was a shining and a piercing of the gathered clouds
of ignorance and showing men their man-Way to Perfection,
the Way of truth and fellowship and lovely art — Himself
the Demonstration of its conclusion; and at the same time
reaffirming to the ant his ant-Way and to birds
bird-Way — to all creatures, He-themselves, Him.
The same Sun was merely the gladness of one, another
it burnt to ashes so that he became God.
The same Wind was a whispering breeze in the sheltered valley,
and a Gale on the tops of the mountains. The same love
to one was a touch in his dream slightly remembered,
to another the Kiss which initiated final union.

21

As Jesus He had to get Himself crucified — since earth is the junction
of heaven and hell — in order to get His words fulfilled and establish
His Word. As Krishna He had to get shot with an arrow and allow

the abduction of the Gopis — since His business had been with arrows
and flute-playing (and beauty is always violated by the world) —
in order to establish love. As Buddha He had to eat poisoned food —
since He was a mendicant begging His food — in order to uphold
His doctrine of transiency and demonstrate compassion to every one
and thing. As Mohammed He had to get stoned — since He lived
as a man among men in a world of stones — in order to establish
in men's hearts democracy. As Baba He has had to get involved
in car accidents — since He has come to a world of machines —
in order to break the backbone of machines' materiality
and establish their proper usage in Man's spiritual life.

22

After Siva, Mahanirvanasutra to take the place
of an obsolete yoga. After Krishna, the Bhagavatas
in order to clean up the Brahmin mess of misunderstood sacrifice.
After Buddha, Socrates and his son Plato
to keep the same-light that was in Homer the pure burning
through the murk that was setting in with the betrayal of Poetry
to the time of Jesus after whom, the desert men living
as Jesus told men to live — naked, homeless, solitary —
all well-forsaken for God in order to counteract priesthood
and political organization and Paul's doctrine of Interference;
and Gregory and Ambrose to link up with the Sufis
who were after Mohammed in order to prevent
the 72 jarring sects from completely obscuring His Word
so that It could again establish lovely art in people's lives.

23

With BABA, "God Speaks"; and His SPEAKING: again Sun
piercing clouds and full shining in clear sky and hearts of men
awakened and lovely Art and her maidens treading their dance
on the green earth and men amazed at the forms and rhythms
of the dance. And *with* Art works and speech and worship
and walking, and the walking of lovers in twilight hushed
with bond-of-Him; and children again being instructed
in the alphabets of love-speech.
And men again marching with battle-songs in the holy war of Self
and conquering and returning and stone-cutting and building
and stripping away the scaffolding of flesh
revealing lovely edifices of His Name. And speech swift as thought
unhampered by labour of words and thought instant with reality.
Earth a carpet of eyes for His feet in the lives of men.

24

Mohammed, the Democrat: There is ONE GOD
and He *is in* your hearts; He alone you should adore
and obey. Hold Him above every thing (and one) else.
And Francis of Assisi was His true Apostle, although he was
calling Him Jesus (out of habit), because he said with Him,
"Poverty is my glory" ("bride" to him) and was a true faqeer,
a one-robed-man, shoeless with clean feet. Then came the Humanists,
deluded that freedom was *outside* themselves — the beginning
of false democracy — who shouted horizons and taught us
to seek a new god, one greater than Mohammed and Jesus
who would not require of us *via dolorosa* and prayer to wipe clean
the mirror for the Image; and whom we easily found
because he was also looking for us. And *line,*
the boundary of the Boundless, became thick with our blood.

25

To what, O teachers of men, are you *bridges* to your pupils?
to Space-men who will rule the earth; bridges
to further-from God. Your teaching has desolated the earth:
shorn the mountains of grandeur, silted the rivers of sweet water
and turned the green places into deserts. The earth
is no longer sufficient sphere for the influence of your power —
now you would inhabit the moon with desolation; set in the skies
the Eye of your god to report men. You have made barren the heart
so that song no longer arises from the people's labour.
You have made intellect feeble, so that their minds
can no longer grasp: GOD ALONE IS; and I *am* HE.
You have dissected Spirit and taught it is merely sense-behaviour.
Bridges indeed you are! bridges to the *last* slavery —
divine Men (Hu-Manas) as automata for automation.

26

You have taught us, who ranged the planes of power,
who *were* the Sons who shouted when the stars danced, to deny
our Father and renounce our heritage — taught us
the non-humanity of desolation: a sneer in the vestibule,
a giggle in the dark, a stare and a blink in the sunlight,
an accounting of figures to take another's life,
a grovelling in dirt to make a machine
to conquer emptiness and destroy ourselves.
The Bright Ones of God ever showed us the Way

to ourSelf, ever held up a mirror in which shone
our loveliness; ever sang to us the cradle-songs
of our Beginning, chanted the story of self-conquest
and Returning and Arrival and Abiding in our own Perfection.
Ever whispered deliciously in our ears: YOU ARE GOD.

27
The greatness of Dante was not in his vision
of the three worlds, but in his experience of Beatrice.
The greatness of Beethoven was not in his symphonic embracements
but in the quartet and piano communings with his beloved.
When love approaches a man he becomes silent
except for "Thou". From "Thou" arises millions of words
or notes which he weaves into patterns pleasing
to his beloved's ear. The world now knows not this art.
There is a Way which the Masters proclaim,
which the saints enjoy, in which the artist,
with the industry of a child, plays, and prattles
the beginning of love-speech. As he grows older his Father
sends him out into the world of the Way where he becomes a hero.
Then gives him work to do by which he becomes an artist of Self.

28
There is no Way without an already-Knower of the Way,
no unveiling from ignorance to Truth without an Unveiler.
Even Avatar requires someone to unveil Him to Himself,
to awaken Him to His Self-appointed divine mission.
It is evident that Jesus was naming John as His Master
when He berated them: What
went you out to see, a reed shaken by the wind?
No man born of woman is greater than he.
And in this saying He was also explaining the difference
between man-God and God-man.
John was a man who had become God;
Jesus was God who had become a man:
both equal in consciousness — both perfectly God —
each with a different role in God's affairs in the world.

29
O Sun! when will
you break through the encircling night of our day,
cherish our hearts, spill

133

gladness and set our feet dancing in your holy Way —
blossom your azure?
O Sun, burn with your diamonds our web of fears —
not our tears
alone our full cup and measureless measure.
O Sun the earth is ripe for budding
new treasure;
the heavens await a new studding
of instant pleasure
of your light for you. When will you break
our sleep and dreaming; our holy feet awake?

30
Food. Food'...The best men of us dreamed of a world
without hunger — but we are very hungry, God.
Our symphonies and cinema and serials and sight-seeing
do not feed us; our social-sciences do not sustain
us in health — we live longer, but with less sap in our sinews.
Hunger. Hunger. From belly-hunger from vitamin lack
to God-hunger from Word and Form in heart lack — and the children
scavenge for crumbs in the garbage-cans of our frustration.
Hunger. Crops of hungers. Hungers for which we have names
and nameless hungers. Our hunger weakens our will to seek food
and causes us to reject whatever morsels of touch and glance
and living culture of other peoples are offered us. Kailas —
thy cut-stone frescoes! — Food. Food.—The food of your Word,
BABA.—The Spear-of-food of your Silence-breaking and SPEAKING.

31
The *science* of the Self; the *art* of Realization:
the only truly human occupation, to teach which, God
descends again and again, suffers our limitation
and allows His own crucifixion. Bright God, bright Brightness
of God — the Beginning, the Course and the End
of all science; the Model, the Maker and the Made-work
of all art — teach us the science of self-forgetfulness,
teach us the art of your Name. Nameless
are we because of names, homeless because of houses;
workless in works, art-less in artifice;
our eyes without sight, our hands without skill,
our ears stopped through the whirr of words and machines.
Sing to us anew your ancient singing,
show us again the pristine loveliness of your Face.

32

Renaissance — the Dawn. Cold dawn from which arose
and shone only a fitful winter sun soon to decline
and leave our world to night — night of coal and oil,
of "noise-level" exchanged for voices and guitars.
But in anticipation of our present time when the wheat of song
would be withered in its roots, we invented the symphony,
and camera and tape-recorder and recorded the folk-song and sculpture
still in the world, so that *we would not know*
that we could no longer hear and see. Cold dawn, short
fitful day, and then black night in which we built
cathedrals to Ares in New York (and other places),
abstracted God to a code of Industrial Ethics
and shook hands and back-slapped our bargain —
and bubble-whizzed to found a New World on the moon.

33

But God is Watchful, Compassionate. He
in the Perfect Five witted the times — the loss
of song in the earth and mirth in men's eyes
and naked Nature weeping in her desolations.
And He brought Himself down wrapped in His divine veil
of form; reared Him with His-mother tenderness;
kissed Him between the eyes, and made Him know
Himself as the Ancient One, Formless, Beyond
all beyonds, All-knowing, All-bliss; and established Him
as His-Avatar for the Salvation of men and Renewal of earth.
Then He hid Himself behind the veils of heart within each one,
within each beast and bird and insect and every atom of matter,
as a sun in winter rising behind cloud-veils
and waiting the time in time to break through in shining.

34

And began calling his disciples and training them to obedience
and inuring them to heat and cold and thirst and sleeplessness;
for great as was our cry and wretchedness,
so great his work, so fit his workers to withstand
our heats of greed, coldness of love and our deserts and night.
He was a Moon of tenderness in their well-being, a Sun
of burning in their tempering — smoothing the troubled lines
of their hearts and melting their souls in attunement.
Then he took them out on the roads — for him, the beginning

of his earth-wanderings, for them to learn they were homeless
and he was their home: in each step he breathed in their breath
his Name till they knew they were Nameless and that Namelessness
has Name; walked in their walk taking their burdens
lightly upon him till they knew they walked with God.

35

Then he erected a scaffolding of hospital and dispensary,
shelters for the migrant and poor and a school of love for boys
for his Building of Selfless Service in men's hearts. And
when the building was completed he removed the scaffolding
and took his disciples out on the road again. This time
he travelled to the outposts of the world, Europe and America
(later, also to Australia), feeding the poor of us — the belly-fat poor
and the God-poor of us wherever he went. Contacted his agents,
for the Americas a Red Indian in New Mexico,
for Europe a man in Rome. He spent a night
in a cave his servant Francis had used — that servant
so beloved that he had made him as perfect as himself
is perfect; and visited Avila (still retaining sanctity)
where John and Teresa had loved and worked for him.

36

And returned to India, where he turned his love towards
the children of God, the saints and masts who live on pavements
and in hovels and by the shelterless wayside — turned his love
to them, as a great teacher and artist returning from public lectures
turns the ripe fulness of his experience and love to his pupils,
his fellow-workers: Shah Ali Nur Pathan (Cha Cha) God-drowned,
wearing a body he didn't know about; Chatti Baba,
moon-singer of glorious song; Karim Baba, sun-man
and ruler; Mohammed, heart-melter with his singing;
Ali Shah, great child who smoked cigarettes continuously;
Phulwala, who wove garlands of flowers and adorned himself,
but a sun-man "who with a slap could take you to sight of God";
Pullukollah, King of Masts, whose reputation was great because
he could cross rivers unaided — but none knew his real authority;

37

Pir Fazal Shah, adept pilgrim, aged but hale, who said, "No one before
has so pierced my heart with love"; Moti Baba, loved and revered
by harlots; Nawab Ali Shah, who gave the disciple presents

when he knew he was God's emissary; Qadir Saheb,
sometimes master, sometimes drowned; Nasiban Mastani
of singing guitars; Mastani Mai, whose eyes were a vina
in adoration of her lord; Maulvi Saheb, Chargeman of Madras;
Waliji, who was ordered to loose Godavari's waters at Nasik
and did so; Gadge Maharaj
who brought Vithoba-Baba to Pandharpur and assembled
70,000 by the river in the moonlight singing in chorus
the praises of the living God. These are the names of a few
of the Sun and Moon men and women whom Baba embraced and
        forwarded
and, he said, worked with in his universal work.

38
Now he entered his Great Seclusion of forty days — Curtain,
in his divine Play, between the two Acts of Glory and Helplessness;
and with the first act established in the hearts of the Audience
in potentiality of being, stepped lightly onto the stage for Act II,
inviting whomso to join him. Those who did must be dead men,
who have no further connection with the living, ask no more questions
and need no provisions for the journey — journey of no-reward,
for love, for dear love. And when the glorious morning of their going
dawned, they set forth gloriously. And they sang a new song,
the Song of Helplessness and Hopelessness. "This is the end
of my beginning and the beginning of my end." And on the pilgrim road
of this Act he enacted, for its establishment in us,
that *trial* which all, who would know Self, must pass through,
the destruction of mind which stands between ourselves and Truth.

39
And when mind was gone, his Old-Life of Knowledge, Strength and
        Greatness
were; but he kept also, by his own act of keeping, the ignorance
and weakness and humility of the New. Then was he at the same time
Himself and us. And so arose in him Life, free and obligationless:
the life of Master and Servant; of knowledge that we are all eternally One,
Indivisible and Infinite in essence, but separate in ignorance;
life of strength in Knowledge and weakness in binding desires.
And this led to the tripartite life of *complicated-free-life* in which
bindings dominated freedom; *full-free-life* in which freedom dominated
bindings; *fiery-free-life* wherein both freedom and bindings were consumed
in the fire of Divine Love. Now was there a complete blending

of God-state and Man-state in which the one lived not in opposition
to the other, neither did one encroach upon the province of the other.
And the divine truth of his realization he shared with those who sought it.

40
Now was the time to say he was the Ancient One, Highest of the High —
which he did. And taught the people and warned them
that if they too thought this, never to ask of him
favours and miracles — they were the whims and duties of saints —
he, as the Lord of Creation, had already appointed what is:
"Seek Me not to put off from you your troubles,
but find Me in order to surrender yourself to Me:
make My happiness your cheer and My comforts your rest.
Do not expect Me to cure your afflictions, but your ignorance. Beg Me not
to save your life, but to permit you to lay down your life at My feet."
Thus he consoled them and encouraged them also to become perfect.
And he called his disciples and workers together at Meherabad,
the first place of his worldly work, for a month to enjoy his company,
for the time was near when he would speak the Word of his *Speaking*.

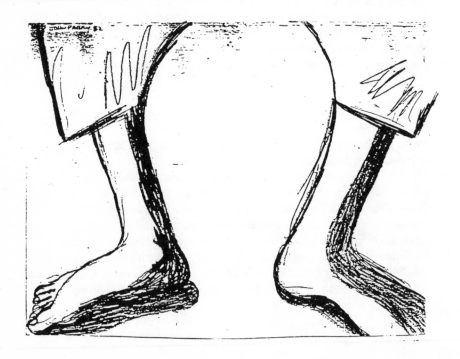

PART IV

1

At Ellura they have cut living memorials to God in stone.
Out of stone God has carved living flesh ready for light —
worm-flesh and fish-flesh and bird-flesh and beast-flesh;
and man-flesh, flesh in His image, He knowable to Himself:
body of matter — gross body
body of energy — subtle body
body of mind — mental body
Mind's daughters, Wisdom and Bliss.
       Dharmakaya of the Eternal One
       Sambodhakaya of Knowledge
       Nirmanakaya of the Perfect Masters:
                    as Tukaram said,
after plunging a knife into his thigh and drawing out cotton-wool,
This is NOT man-flesh as *you* know man-flesh.

2

Cut Self in stone-image of hard contrariety — separation.
Cut from residual impressions of stone, metal-image ...
up to Man. From man-image, cut away dross of impressions
revealing Self-image.—The planesmen along no roads but themselves
adoring this Self: us, weeping mist-veils of further flesh —
wave-beating and land-roving, seeking light:
sweating our brother and examining the drops for light;
cutting his throat and examining the drops for light;
selling and procuring our sisters and examining their tears for light.
And God, His-Avatar, He-the-Perfect Masters, He in the saints, saying,
"Journey is returning.
Light is in your own sweat sweated for neighbour,
in your own blood shed for him,
in your own tears wept for his comfort."

3

Wave-CREATING and beating and 3 worlds-banner planting
through 7 Kingdoms to divine-shape-man and Self-knowledge
(answer to "Who am I?") possible — the Mirror fashioned,
and the Image, conceived of lovely Art, framed therein. BUT
wave-beat of sea-lanes and flag planting earth-portions
of dusty earth; and the Image covered by man-image
of hopes and terror and distance

shaped in contours of CALLING of oar-pull
and revved engines and sun-glare and moon solace of night-white
smooth flesh. And, at last, relinquishing his image. AND
wave-beating the shining planes' roads and the Image
asserting in clearer and clearer outline. And FINAL drowning.
AND A ROAD back for a few to be Men-God, so that the Road is kept open
for God man-illusioned to become Realized.

4

Stone-shape and metal-shape and plant-shape and worm-shape
and fish-shape and bird-shape and beast-shape is out-marching
of God. Man-shape is outpost and returning.
A man is a man when he is seized of God
and seizes himself and repents distance and regards
men-march and men-conquest as children's unkind games,
and further births as indulgence and tedium
and turns back; and takes his first step in heroism
of "not-this" of anything I am or know
and seeks the Perfect Master, the Awakener, the Deliver, and keeps not
himself in any degree for himself, but offers the lot, the lot,
and becomes a child and through service and prostration
assumes tallness and man-ness and acquires knowledge.

5

Thirst: earth-thirst for rain; men-thirst for man-shape;
planesmen's thirst for light; saint-thirst for God.
Birth is where thirst may be slaked, and new thirst
thirsted — until the last-thirst is drowned in Union.
The rains are according to the lips of the earth, the mouths of roots:
therefore Hafiz said, "Cry not because of thirst,
but to create more." In nature there is never erosion,
nor is rain spilt by an ungrateful earth.
The rain of the lover's kisses awakens wells of response
in the loved one; it is the light from his eyes
which causes her eyes to become a mirror for him
to behold love. Cry to create thirst
so that you may become the loved one of love,
so that you may become the recipient of His kisses.

6

No Dark Ages. Everything known by the first man who learnt
to dance inside himself, in the centre of the earth, in the sun —
the world and the universes spinning around him: true 3-dimensionalism.

Prajapati taught it to Manu, Manu to ... up to
the present living perfect men who, with Jesus
were before Abraham and Prajapati: cut it in Anuradhapura stone,
in Ellura stone, for all men to read.
Wave-beat and land-roved West to come out East:
to America to discover cities built in the sunrise by lover-craftsmen
who reckoned precious stones as ornaments for Him-
escaped-from-stone; to the Pacific for Fenollosa to demonstrate
the migration of "motive" to China (B.C. 3000-250);
so that Jesus-lovers could make "Santos" in New Mexico,
so that Ares'-worshippers could build cathedrals in New York.

7

Wave-beat it to immeasureable removes from God-Man,
the Artist — quest of our journeying: pouring our blood
before numberless altars of Christ-Ares-Aphrodite,
burning our flesh as savour for his-gods heathen to us:
arctic remove from Sun-belt of shining, flight to stars
from flight under shadow of His-swan motionless in the empyrean,
dead-seas wave-beat from Ocean-of-drowning —
sculpture without Zen, painting without Pragña,
verse without Breath vivifying. Thy works are poison
withering all things green; thy stratospheric nosing
exudes stench thrusting God ever and ever further back
from thy teeming presence. Immeasurable removes,
misery infinitely extensionable — irretraceable
except His-God-Man sufferance of our sin.

8

Let's do it man-shape.—WOT
man-shape ? — MY man-shape, of course. I
the creator. In My-shape and be — to you.—
Let's do it bit Japanese-like ? bit Persian-like ?
bit Negro-like ? Let's make it *Ethnic*. And
make up sentences: energy is the mountain ...
another dot changes the relation ... seership through hallucination. ...
You write me a letter (for publication) and I'll write you.—
Are you writing your autobiography ? — Let's write in
Greek and Latin and French and Chinese for us to read in English.—
My way — NOT Way-way of
Art-way of Tang-way and Toltec-way and Kailas-way and Assisi-way —
obliteration of self through tears-way, the dust-way
of the devotees on the path to God.

9

After we had looked out and dog-sniffed horizons
we had to invent false perspective in order
to free ourselves from the "tyranny" of Truth,
and develop an "ethic" of *space* (humanism) and SOMEHOW
hook up "Christ" with Ares flat-footed god of flat
earth-sprawl and his playful bedfellow NOT
ocean-born goddess of God, mother of Eros
Murshid of men to God. And train scholars
to write a history of achievement from no-date
of Avatar Jesus, and a 2-dimensional Scripture for us,
for the pagans still lost in 3-dimensional dance
whose sweat we required for extraction
of boudoir perfumes and steak condiment. AND that
we could ultimately make I.C.B.M., and rule from the moon.

10

Make it new. New as sun rising and leaf-green,
New as lover's complaint and journey and union,
New as the sacrifice of touch and eyes and speech,
the virgin's sacrifice, the mother's; New as earth bearing.
New as Paul's "Are men still building cities?"
as Njal's "God will not require one to suffer fire twice",
as Gunnar's wondering why he was not "brisk" as other men,
as Chatti Baba's wondrous sweet singing.
Wamadeva said, "*I* am New. New is My glory, My Eternality."
New are the wars of Troy and Kurukshetra,
New the Ram of Abraham, the Lamb of Jesus;
New is God, His-Avatar in ever Sameness,
New are the acts creative of the Perfect Masters,
New are the conversations of the saints with God.

11

Yer might know how it goes, Mr. Picasso,
but unless yer cun get yerself outa the way and do it fer God
yer goin' ter finish up talkin' ter yerself and yerself not knowin'
wot yer talkin' about. Different from "old-men's talk", i.e.
intuitive perception by/in mature mind of reflection of
light-outline-of-Beloved, and stating it in self-intimate terms
of universal applicability self-pleasing and BECAUSE
God might also be getting a kick out of it.
There is a little flame in the heart,

shrouded in smoke which reddens the eyes to squint-seeing,
or clear which burns up self-rubbish so that sight becomes keen
and the path opens to Art and saintship. Either gets fanned
according to the little wind yer breath makes, Mr. Picasso.
. . . And Ezra Pound an old man too without old-man's singing.

12

Ideograms: draw a vertical line. Down this we came
in search of answer to our question *"Who* am I?"
Draw a horizontal line across the bottom — rock-bottom.
Metal-bodied, metal-brained. Plant-, worm-,
fish-, bird-, beast-, man-bodied, brained.
Man-bodied, man-brained — the goal of form — full consciousness
of gross-world (finiteness) — ROCK-BOTTOM, terminus
and turning point. Raise up the horizontal line
and begin the glory road through the 6 planes of singing.
The two lines now also the cross of Crucifixion.
On the 5th plane the real singing begins — the secondary art (devotion).
On the 6th plane the divine love play of lover and Beloved.
The top is the 7th plane, where both lines vanish. Actually
they were never marked by you on the paper.

13

Wave-beating, we were, and arm-waving in attitudinization —
buckets of mud and symphonic oceania and spires of New York
probing the night promised us as dawn.
But Song never dies. Here and there
its green eyes pushed up through the bitumen and concrete
and looked around looking for the Son of God,
for light, for nourishment.
But fatness comes not to the earth-bellied ones
through the poet's art, nor "progress"
through the lisping of those learning love speech,
and they knew how to deal with them —
hunger, ridicule, imprisonment, indifference,
or the firing-squad
in the pale dawn. Dawn, the nourisher.

14

Contemptible scholarship — which is not used
to prove intellectually the *fact* of God;
which bows not before the lovely acts of the saints,

which fouls the springs of Art;
which eats bread and uses houses,
which feeds none
and consumes the hand that ploughs and builds;
which causes pain in sweat, encourages
forgetfulness in leisure
so that none repeats the Name of God in secret
nor chants in unison of praise in family circle.
Contemptible scholarship — your "not-this" is your own not-Self.
If it were not for Dante's blunder
One might be tempted to paint for you a special hell.

15
Light. Light in a loaf of bread baked with love;
light in a cup of water in the name of God's poverty;
tear-light and sweat-light and eye-light
shining out through crack in heart walls.
Wave-beating and land-roving for light; digging in earth
examining stone, metal, for light, examining
the shadows of form, the forms of shadows, words, sound
for light. Light of the saints nourishing Art.
Light of the Perfect Masters supporting the world and directly piercing
heart and awakening soul to journeying, and God-bestowing.
Light of Avatar in all things — ant-light, tree-light,
man-light — cutting their paths for them. After Him,
the beginning of poetry and stone-cutting to commemorate light —
to feed our daily lives. Light. Light the dream. Light the Reality.

16
Wouldn't it be a wonderful thing to have a friend
who wouldn't want one to beguile time
but would turn on one in kindly anger, "You bloody loafer —
whatya foolin' about *doing* instead of being occupied with His Name?"
Who would bang on one's door in the middle of the night,
"Up there, lizard! wastin' ya life in sleep and dreaming."
Who would mock one's hypocrisy and posturings
and laugh his sun-laugh at one's shadow-earnestnesses.
A friend of knowledge, who, when he spoke, you would be listening
to little songs; and when he was silent, you felt home-sickness
as though you both came from the same Place. Who,
before the final courteous closing of his door (when he would be
wholly about his Father's business) sang you a special song
which would break open in an intense flower the secret of music.

17

The greater war in the service of Self — Existence, Knowledge, Bliss;
the lesser war, fighting for passingness, ignorance and rebirth.
The greater war — wearing gross-impressions out into subtle-impressions;
wearing subtle-impressions out into mental-impressions;
wearing mental-impressions out: Self where He is
and no-*where* else. The lesser war of gregarious sweat and fear —
fear of a footstep going, coming, of the newspaper and telephone,
of a strange hat or perfume in the hallway,
of rain of red death from the skies.
The General of one, the "Thus-come" of Jesus-now-BABA;
of the other, the god of thy gods, incestuous Ares.
On the one hand, I am my own enemy;
on the other, Feed me my greed, or die.
The Song of Sun-farer; the snarled curse in the dark.

18

Wrapped in veils of custom and costume
we imagine our little war is the real war. We are habited
to the discomfort of comfort, never having savoured Jetsun's
Song of Comforts — never believing that love is better than wine.
Our Father's house is seven-storied — V-style,
the ancient architecture. We crowd the ground floor —
some to the front rooms overlooking the park,
some to the back rooms on the lane of garbage-cans.
The custom — the comforts. The costume —
a little seven-piece, seven coloured affair (see "God Speaks"
for details) cut according to sex,
class, occupation and ambition, costing
from avidya one lakh upwards, depending on
fastness of dye, depth of hue and unwashableness.

19

Jetsun didn't like it — chose angel's breath instead.
Moses didn't like it — preferred home-spun wool.
Chaitanya and Chishti clothed themselves in song;
Kalyan in devotion; Sadashiv in silence;
John in strangerhood; Francis in poverty;
Sankaracharya, and Plato (whom Jili "saw" filling the world with light)
in reason beautiful; Junaid put on the dress of "manner";
Laotze wove his from the thread of Emptiness.
Kabir, a poet who was God — and so knew all about it — said:

"Open the folds of your Veil and you shall find God."
Hafiz, another poet who also was God said,
"You yourself are the cover over Self and you haven't got a chance
of taking yourself off so that you can see you
unless you become dust under the feet of a Perfect Master."

20
Dust, the dress suitable for mendicants and lovers to whom
Isaiah was especially speaking when he said, "Awake! and sing."
Meaning, that they who had voluntarily made themselves as dust,
it was their turn now to become clothed in lovely song.
From dust God made the first man.
In dust Majnun found Leila.
With dust Chatti Baba blest the reverent.
With dust and spit Abdul Jilani healed the leper.
Eden was an island of green-ness —
no dirt, no chance
of real singing there — only angel-chants of praise.
So its down the dusty road of separation
and hard yakker and sweat —
the royal road to Song.

21
Out-marching is dreaming movement and recoil
each night to sleep; action's drag-chain
dead-slowing the feet to standstill and the sting of its rub
rousing again to world and failure or success
in new journeying. "Yer know, they actually
work all day and sleep all night!" Work is in stillness
in the Name of God. The Real-dreaming men sleep little —
"one hour is enough for a fighter"— and "take no thought
for that which is every moment perishing."
Meditate, or be damned;
love, or be lost in the roads (and at each end) of rebirth.
Out-marching is keeping the Wheel of Birth
turning. Sitting down doing nowt but love
is slowing the blasted thing to its ultimate stopping.

22
Dream-progress thy works —"Cunning contrivance
makes for cunning performance" of cunningly wrought
vehicle of dream-experience: drop of spray of Ocean
falling and calling in 7-coloured rainbows and proclaiming

146

falling and calling is direction.
Big dream of God-dream;
little dreams of men-dream —
the dream freshening, and turning stale, diminishing; clear
outline, edges vague, shape lost and hope it returning
or a new lovelier one. "Once . . ."
Big Wheel and little wheels. And up yer go
and down yer come because that's the way yer want it.
Being a mean man you do not wish to obey the seasons
let alone find the Unvarying. Being a mean man . . .

23
Once our acts were act.
But action darkens the blood and makes it heavy
and heaviness breeds anger. But always we turned
in repentance and returned and relit
the sacrifice and relearned the name of the Word,
and took up anew the ancient labour chants.
Every time was this so since Siva
in His eternal meditation on Kailas was touched by Parvati
to bring us the first of the new Scriptures.
We sang his Compassion in the works of our hands
and protected the earth in its seasons.
We taught our children dancing and poetry.
And built temples in our hearts and in the land
adorned with pictured stories of His love.

24
We carved God out of stone and saints
out of our flesh. And the stone sang
and the saints showed us the way of work and journeying.
Easy it was for us to worship stone, even
the work of our hands, since He dwelt in it again —
He, Great God, not diminished of His greatness;
He, the Friendly, staying with us, accepting the milk of our offering
through His stone lips vivified by our perfect saints.
Stone was His first habitation —
the saints are his perfect and last.
So we reverenced the saints and never ate
without first offering them food for their fasting;
never slept without making sure of a bed
for their nights of sleepless adoration and conversation with God.

25

Always we returned from the little war
and took up the great war and our duty
of song and stations of singing.
Then they, our blood, told us of a God
easier to worship who would give us power
over men, over earth, over sun.
And we denied our hands and the saints and exiled ourselves
and forgot courtesy and speech and singing.
A lonely exile: a weary wave-beating,
a sullen sojourn slipped of sympathy and communion —
herding like cattle in drought toward mirage pasture;
standing like ruined timber against a skyline
nor even remembering sun and the flow of sap and surging green.—
And built cathedrals . . .

26

". . . to pay attention to his own self rather than to his activities."
Who will for Christ's sake stop jigging about
and sit down in himself and start journeying,
stop bickering and "become aggressive to himself". Or
no art, no established peace, no acquisition of real knowledge.
No chance of "heart-tone", of "season";
of the other person called Woman wanting to give you
her most fine and most delicate and release you
to planesmanship instead of swamps-binding.
Only by the Boundless may boundary be defined,
by non-solid, density determined.
To pay attention — to come to rest, stay at rest;
Stay with God . . . Or ever thy Kali-tongues insatiable
in the cavern of going and coming.

27

Stay outside as the dog which you are. Accept with love
the food given you by God. And when spirit groweth faint
and heart cries out for love-morsel, remember the Secure Ones
houseless, their outstretched palm their begging bowl.
"Be brave!" O brave one, retreat into His Name
and proclaim in your heart you are That — and soon
or later, the door to His presence will swing open.
They whose companionship you would seek, are hungry —
they bicker one another looking for love; homeless are they.
Eat apart from them and feed them.

Remain separate and draw them together.
Give them back the fire they have stolen from their hearths.
Feed them and draw them after you
through the Door you have found to Heaven.

28
Shatter
the distance-mirror which reflects
self in histrionic inconsequences —
art adolescent, burden on bread.
Long enough to and fro about the earth and returning
without profit or messages — to and fro,
dogs sniffing tufts of grass and lamp-posts
for scent of dogs; long enough backsides up
in piano proclamation and choral belligerances.
We are beyond tears and humanity.
We are alone each one in his own hell-night
of burning which we must suffer
until we ask pardon and beg His waters of healing
and drowning. Only "O God ! O God !"
can break this night in fresh morning of New Day.

29
When a man gets to 40 years
he must start to think — or perish. Face himself
in his opinions and conceits, his attitudes and posturings.
It will take him 10 years to achieve even a little honesty
and weaning. By then he will find
there is not a soul who can exert even a little finger
to help him — he is alone with himself — and *somewhere* a journey.
He is then 50, ready to begin earnest idleness,
to fit himself for love — to begin the adult occupation.
Ambition turning into resignation; loves turning into love;
thoughts forming into tangible concept. Mind coming to rest;
body comfortable, mind coming to rest — impressioned
of joy, reflecting joy. World,
the morning mist dissolving before the sun of His loveliness.

30
Hunger is habit — mind-habit of belly, eye, ear and touch.
Hunger is habit of burning: fire from the hearth —
gift of Agni-Prometheus to ignite devotion,
to consume the obstacles to freedom — stolen

for camp-fires of journeying escaped into the bush
engulfing farmsteads and farmlands:
fire which feeds on sweat and careful anxiety.
Fire patterning night with brightness,
diminishing distance and making comfort seem nearer:
leaping from hilltop to hilltop
across lands and seas, chain-beacon
messaging victory and mean death: fire
which now may only be extinguished
by the living grace of the living Master.

31
Unless a man stops buzzing and feeding on flesh
and shuts his mouth, his mouth will never become sweet
for arm-bangled Sophia's kisses; nor will
lovely daughters be born to him to come to lovely womanhood
and cheer his old age with wine and companionship.
He will never come to cave-habitation, but must bear the discomfort
of house-dwelling, distrusted by birds and beasts,
uncourtesied by weather and seasons,
unworshipped by sun, unadorned by stars or stones.
Shuts his mouth so that Mind, pregnantly impressioned
of God, reflects only through hue of flesh
and gait of hand and foot and clear-eyed love-glancing —
reflection of idle self in silence
intensely adoring blissful silent Self.

32
A man will journey so far, and then quietly
or in a heroic spasm examine what he has collected
and say with Gunnar: This is my fall. Now
I will not journey anywhither to satisfy obsolete law.
Fair is my house set fair in the meadows,
and the corn ripe to harvest.
Soon will this house be laid in ruins
under great battle, and she whom my soul loved
betray me for small spite.
Great glory there would be for me in fulfilment of their law,
but I, undefeated yet in fight,
am weary of men's honour and am called by God
to the battlefield of Sigurd and the other great heroes
pressing strenuously the way back to our Father.

33
Adore adorative Self, the God-Man, the Artist —
Who strove us the stages of stone-shape and plant-shape
worm, fish, bird and beast to man-shape,
and broke through the seas of form, energy, thought-feeling
to Self-state and returned to us with form illumining all forms.
Adore adorative Self, the path-Breaker,
He, God, He-the-Gods
of creation, preservation and dissolution;
the form-Moulder, the quality-Imbuer,—
the Teacher of lovely form, the Teacher of right quality — the Artist;
the Skill of thy hand, the Energy of thy motive,
the Thought of thy conception: thy Self's
setting out and returning to forward your going.
The saints feed you; but the God-Man makes you God.

34
Adore adorative Self — the Glorious-one. Sun
of sun coming up out of ocean and giving glory
to the hills and light to all being's purposes.
Sun of clear sky and cloud-flowered sky,
Sun of grass-plains and forests and bird-song
and wheat and groves and vineyards.
Sun of men journeying for gold and God —
lighting the land paths and sea lanes and Involution's Gate
guarded by swords and the eyes of chaste women.
Sun of the planes to God — of the clear way and the entrancements.
Sun of wisdom and knowledge;
of the saint's adoration and love-speech.
Sun of your pristine Self wrapping all beings
in an unequal world equally in glory.

35
Adore adorative Self: the Shy-one veiled in form
looking out from behind the lattice of world
waiting for heart-calling for empty hearts to inhabit.
The Helpless-one — crawl-in-worm-One,
rooted-in-earth-One growing His own tree of crucifixion;
the helplessly-shining-One in cut diamonds,
helpless-in-wings-One prisoned in prey search,
helpless-in-beast-One lowing crop-hunger.
The Beggar-one on the roads begging bread, gold,

fairness of vision, women, intellect, friendship,
the skies and seas for knowledge; begging the Road back.
The Beggar on the planes begging light, love, entrancement,
freedom from entrancement; on the last plane
begging love's union, begging Self's being of Self.

36

When we have ceased from the noise of expression — Come the day;
when we no longer require compensative action for inadequacy
and have progressed to watchful idleness — Come the day;
a little bell will shine in heart-sky in summons
to journeying, and a smiling Sophia will teach us lovely art.
And the gods of He-the-One-God, Athene
and Apollo and Poseidon and Ganesh and Surya and Saraswati
will teach us the poetry of effective words
and the music that makes rain fall in correct abundance
and dancing that delights animals and wheat;
teach us stone-cutting, how to cut His Name in stone
so that stone will again shine with His light
and sing — teach us to make stone images
that will drink milk from our hands.

37

For God is Watchful, Compassionate and in the Five
witted the times and brought Him, His-Avatar down.
And nurtured Him
through infancy and childhood and youthhood
and with a kiss unveiled Him and with a stone
enknowledged Him with His own knowledge
and gave over to Him His own world
for its awakening and fresh path-setting.
And He has become us, our poorest us, even
the most outposts-of-the-poor-of-us and assumed
our hopelessness and become our helplessness
and fed us with the Bread of His continuous Crucifixion . . .
Of His eyes, our light; of His touch, our works;
and of His Silence our again-speaking in terms of lovely Art.

38

And also caused to be written down "God Speaks" in English
as though He'd got tired of Sanskrit and Greek and Arabic
and thought He'd say it in the language of the most-gross conscious,
most-straightened people in the earth at the moment.

A Book of a book — delightful (one imagines) to Him
of Way-reminiscence, tedious (since He likes marbles) in explanation —
setting out clearly the stages to here-dumbness, the stages
to There-reality of true man-ness in Existence, Knowledge, Bliss.
A book showing clearly that a mouse cannot know the way
of a Camel, that the Hare and Lion have their own sort of mastery;
that your real troubles only begin when you begin the path
and that you don't really know what love is until you *see* God
and so actually experience your separation.
A book, every page, line, teeming with "Here am I."

39
A book of, I am you and you are Me in eternal Oneness.
Reap the wind of My spirit and the breath of My presence.
Forget, starve into non-being yesterday's harvest
and tomorrow's promise of reaping; sufficient is the day of today
and My *here* with you. Yesterday you were alone;
tomorrow is My speaking and release and your desolation.
Today is your yesterday's millions of years; tomorrow need not occur
if you grasp today in your two willing hands and surrender to Self
and obey Me.—A book of, Love Me, love Me.
Give Me some little part of you — some little cherished sin
or despised virtue, making for Me a small place
in you to live — a small SPACE a bit clean
and free of other company, for I am shy to knock
where I am not wanted and where there is no room for Me.

40
I am the Honey of all things, the Sweetener and Sustainer of hearts
and lives. I assume your limitations, yet I am eternally
pinioned in motionless freedom. I become the most helpless of you
yet My glory is not known even by perfect saints.
I become the most ignorant among you, yet I am Knowledge Absolute.
Of the poor, I am the poorest, yet My bliss is infinite. My life
you easily take, yet I am Eternal Existence Itself.
Yesterdays and tomorrows are waves rolling to and from My NOW.
Stone-dream and worm-dream and fish-dream and bird-dream
and beast-dream and man-dream is My Dream,
and AWAKE-AWARENESS of no dream nor ever was dreaming.
From Awakeness I call you to awaken from man-dream and woman-
      dream,
from gainloss-, despairhope-dream — whispering in your heart-ear
in tones of reverberating thunder My message of silent love.

Coda:

Art is a dreaming between deep sleep and awaking —
God dreaming the creation and dream-answering
the initial question "Who am I?" through evolutionary, involutionary
stages to Knowledge of I AM MYSELF. In us
He dreams our daily lives as little dreams
within the Nothingness of DREAM, and calls the actions of these dreams
and their representation in song and pictures, art —
God, fully conscious, dreaming He is Man.
The real Art of God is His-Avatar assuming
the appearance of a man to wake men from the illusion of appearance.
The real art of men is modelling their flesh
upon the pattern of His perfect Manhood,
dreaming His loveliness and truth, and delineating
in work and works the dreamed Image of His Reality.

Art is the DREAMING between deep sleep and Awakeness
in which God fashioned the universe,
lost Himself in them dreaming they were real, wore out
the successive levels of the dream and awoke in Only-Real-Self.
And, perfectly awake, returned in man-appearance
to Himself in men still dreaming;
returned as Beast, as Bird, as Fish, as Worm
to He in them still dreaming; to light
them in their progress to Himself — infinitely compassionate
that they should STAY with Him
in the most fruitful shape He had patterned
and most easy course He had set — He having proved
all possible shapes and courses —
to stay with God since none, except in dream, exists but God.

Art is the love of God, His-Avatar towards men
shining self-evident-Existence in the midst of seemingness
as sun through mist-veils revealing patterned landscape
of hills and farms and township where none were;
awaking in men love, and they in love
cutting their lives and works in design he lays down,
as a stone-cutter stone fitly for house
well conceived in dimension by master-architect.
Stay with God in whatever shape He shapes you

and work your works within the boundaries of that shape.
Art is His shape of you singing light through your hands,
through your speech, imaging His Image. STAY WITH GOD.
Let the *Dream* dream out the staying and the going of your form
or million forms — they are not you who ever stays with God.

Art is the act of God — the action of His *likeness*
in our hearts: so that we wake from sleeping and begin to dream
of thousands of Brightnesses and lovely Form, and our faces
grow pale and our bodies thin with love. And we wake
from dreaming and behold His lovely Face, and sleep
within His breast and know His thought — and all the world
is lost, well lost. And we wake again and know
that He and I are One — were One and always shall be.
Stay with God. Put down your pen and cease your songs.
Works are for men of love. Not yet has he unsealed His lovely lips
and spoken that Word by which devotion will again be possible.
Still is His Sun hidden behind the curtains of the dawn,
still is His Lion caged from rampancy and glory.
It is for another generation, BABA, to tell your delightful story.
            IN GRIEF, IN JOY, IN DEEPEST GRIEF.

So have I writ what love told me to write,
And every line betrays my poverty
Of love, as a poor man asked his charity
Displays a single shilling to our sight.
Yet I'm somewhat contented of my plight
In that rich love stooped down to ask of me —
Thus honouring me in whom no others see
Worth, myself, the least. Thus does love with light
And gentle grace encourage on his way
The least of us: taking each by the hand
He's laboured with, using the same labour
To raise him to still greater favour —
Even perhaps to love's own path: to stand
In light when Silence *speaks* its shining Day.

Notes

These notes are for readers not familiar with
the general subject matter of this book, and/or
have not read anything of a particular literature to which reference is made or having once
read have since forgotten it.

Preface

This is not to say a real artist is not automatically and instantly a teacher in his very
act of being artist. Real art is in itself the highest teaching. One who has attained
Self-realization is a Perfect Artist in himself whether or not he ever opens his mouth
to others. His very presence among men is a teaching to them of what they should
and may become. After Realization he may remain silent; he may sing in verse the
fact of Truth and describe the stages and states approaching It and comment on
the persons involved in them in order to encourage others to seek Truth as did
Hafiz; or he may, like Sankaracharya, analyse non-Truth in order to prove to the
others the existence of Truth. Each one of them would be no more or no less an
artist than the others.

[*Numerals refer to page number then line: 19/1 = page 19 line 1.*]

Book I

19/1   *Kailas:* a mountain in the Himalayas and mythological seat of Siva. For
description of this mountain and something of its significance, see *The Holy Moun-
tain* by Bhagwan Shri Hamsa, translated by Shri Purohit Swami, Faber & Faber
Ltd., London, 1934; *Kailas Manasarovar* by Swami Pranavananda, S.P. League Ltd.,
Calcutta, 1949.
19/2   *Siva:* the Supreme Lord. In mythology is usually linked with Brahma and
Vishnu. In spiritual tradition he is Adi-Guru, the First Master and World Teacher.
       Ganga: the river Ganges. In mythology Ganga was once in heaven. Saint
Bhagiratha, by his prayers, brought her down to earth. Siva, in order to save the
earth from the shock of the fall of the waters, broke their fall on His head.
       Parvati: Consort of Siva. To people who have been "educated out of" even
belief in the existence of God, the idea of Him having a consort or "wife" may be
"quaint" and belonging to a "primitive" period of Man; and to those brought up
on, and intellectually weakened by, a vague Monotheism linked with a never-
intelligently explained Trinity, rather shocking. But when Parvati is understood as
Sakti, i.e. "wife" equals creative energy, it will be seen that "she" does not in any
sense constitute a modification of "One without a second".
19/4   *Rama, Krishna, Abraham, Zarathustra, Buddha, Mohammed:* Avatars
(Christs) of God.
19/11   *Perfect Master (Sanskrit, Sadguru):* pure, highest absolute teacher; Arabic,
Qutub — Axis, in the sense of Axis of the universe and all life and persons; hence
"all objects and beings are equidistant from Him". One who has realized, in actual
experience, himself as Self or achieved God-consciousness and "returned" to normal, or the ordinary human-conscious state, while retaining without break his
continuous experience of himself as Self or God (Power Absolute, Knowledge Absolute, Bliss Absolute). This "returning" is solely for the purpose of helping "others"
enmeshed in false identification to realize themselves as Self — he has no further
experience or benefit to gain by "coming back". For details see *God Speaks* by
Meher Baba, Dodd, Mead & Co., New York, 1955.

19/12   *saintship:* the real meaning of the word "saint" has become lost through the cessation in the West of the existence of such persons. Throughout this book it is used to denote one who has mastered and transcended in consciousness the worlds of Matter-Energy and the consciousness-functions of the intellect and intuition and is established in direct perception of Truth. There are recognized degrees of experience and authority of saints — the perfect saints enjoying continuously the sight of God "face to face". The Science of the Self or the Science of Planes of Consciousness, no less than the physical Sciences, has its exact terminology. The subject is treated fully in *God Speaks.*

19/15   *Vyasa:* Krishna Dwaipayana Vyasa, the author of the epic Mahabharata in which is told the story of the deeds of Krishna and of which the popular Bhagavad Gita is a section.

Homer: the author of the epics of *Iliad* and *Odyssey.*

Valmiki: the author of the epic Ramayana which tells of the life and deeds of Rama. Valmiki, from being a cut-throat, became after a meeting with a Sage, a devotee of the Name of God. After many years of continuous repetition of this Name, the Ramayana was revealed to him. He is an example of the ideal artist.

19/24   *love now is sealed:* reference to the Mohammedan belief that Mohammed was the last and final Avatar (Arabic, Rassool).

19/30   *Sakyamuni — the Buddha:* derived from Sakya, a warrior tribe which derives its origin from the Sun and in which tribe Buddha was born; and Muni, one who fearlessly faces sorrow, who is not intoxicated with the delight of happiness, and has no fear or the least trace of anger. It is a peculiarity of Buddhism in general that it seems content with the status of Muni for its Master, instead of declaring Him Avatar. In this it is as unenterprising as Mohammedanism which restricts Mohammed to the role only of "Messenger", and has no parallel elsewhere in "Hinduism" or the Sanatan Dharma (The Eternal Religion). The Christians, though restricting Jesus to *one* Advent, at least give Him the credit of being Avatar! although their capitalizing His "miracles" does reduce Him to the status of a mere fourth-planer. On this Meher Baba one day said, "Jesus was God. (*I* ought to know!) As God He was the Creator of the whole universe. How they belittle Him by even mentioning His miracles." The word Sakyamuni is used in this present text to distinguish the historical Buddha from the twenty-four pre-historical Buddhas.

20/1   *Pallas Athene:* in mythology a goddess who was born fully grown and fully armed as a warrior from the head of Zeus the supreme god. As loving Counsellor and Friend, see *Iliad* and *Odyssey.*

20/2   *Telemachus:* son of the hero Odysseus. See *Odyssey.*

Apollo: god of song and music. Also Helper and Destroyer.

20/4   *Chaitanya:* a Perfect Master born in Bengal in the sixteenth century who preached the Way of Devotion to God.

20/5   *Sankaracharya:* a Perfect Master, born in S. India in the eighth or ninth century, who used the method of reason to prove the existence of God (Sanskrit, Paramatman).

20/9   *Krishna, whose flute:* the most loved forms of Krishna are the naughty and merry Child, and the divine Flute-player who entrances all by the beauty of His person and music which awakens in men's hearts the divine song of their own true being. As the latter He is the tangible yet ever elusive Lover for whom the soul longs for intimacy and union.

20/24   *Hafiz:* a Perfect Master in Persia in the fourteenth century who portrayed in flawless verse the divine Truths and the states of relationship between the lover and the Beloved. So far the "Nicholson" of Hafiz has not appeared and most translations are pretty impossible, but there is an excellent small book, *Hafiz of Shiraz,* translated by Peter Avery and John Heath-Stubbs, in the "Wisdom of the East Series", published by John Murray, London.

20/33   *"Poverty is My glory":* a saying of Mohammed.

21/15   *inconceptual experience:* Nirvikalpa Samadhi or "I am God" state. See *God Speaks.*

21/16   *worlds, gross, subtle and mental:* physical universe, the Energy which activates energy-matter and Mind in which they are given existence in illusion.

21/25   *seven planes:* see *God Speaks.*

triple-garment: Mind, Energy and Matter.

21/29   *"The time was Jesus . . .":* Mathnawi by Jelaluddin Rumi. See Note 28/8.

21/35   *Sariputta:* one of the disciples of Buddha.

25/3   *House of the Master:* the place was called "Manzil-e-Meem" or "House of M": the letter "M" (Meem) in Persian being given the significance of one descending from zero. Hence in English, House of the Master.

27/8   *Tilopa:* a Master in N. India in the tenth century.

Naropa: became the Guru of Marpa the translator, a Tibetan who founded the Kargyupta School in Tibet, and whose disciple Jetsun Milarepa, became its most famous Master. This School is still active and functioning according to Marco Pallas in his *Peaks and Lamas.* For the teachings of this School, the only available books in English are the four excellent volumes by W. Y. Evans-Wentz and published by Oxford: *Tibet's Great Yogi Milarepa, Tibetan Yoga and Secret Doctrines, The Tibetan Book of the Dead,* rendered into English by Lama Kazi Dawa-Samdup; and *The Tibetan Book of the Great Liberation,* translated by Sardar Bahadur S. W. Laden La, C.B.E., F.R.G.S., and by the Lamas Karma Sumdhon Paul, Lobzang Mingyur Dorje and Kazi Dawa-Samdup.

It is interesting to note the alteration of "method" of these Masters. Tilopa treated Naropa extremely harshly. Naropa was gentleness itself in his training of Marpa. Marpa's upbringing of Milarepa seemed pitiless; while Milarepa in turn gave his disciples every consideration. The reasons for these differences and especially the reason for his own treatment of Milarepa are beautifully and most touchingly explained by Marpa in *Tibet's Great Yogi Milarepa.*

27/27   *Swigging plonk:* drinking wine.

28/8   *Jelaluddin:* Jelaluddin Rumi, a Perfect Master born in Persia and afterwards settled in Asia Minor (thirteenth century). His works, *The Mathnawi of Jalalu'ddin Rumi,* Luzac & Co., *Divani Shamsi Tabriz,* translated by R. A. Nicholson, Cambridge, *The Rubaiyat of Jalal Al-Din Rumi,* translated by A. J. Arberry, Emery Walker Ltd., were all written after his "Perfection". There is a handy size selection by Nicholson in *Rumi, Poet and Mystic,* Allen & Unwin, in their "Ethical and Religious Classics of the East and the West".

The unflinching loyalty and implicit obedience to a Master even in the face of physical ill-treatment, which is required of an aspirant on the path to Self-knowledge, is difficult for the "Western mind", groping as it is towards Freedom and caught in the ideals of "freedoms" which are only its shadow, to appreciate. Yet our "Authorities" have no hesitancy in imposing unflinching loyalty and implicit obedience on us in the case of National Emergencies, and, after an initial period of "rebellion", we have no difficulty in accepting the necessity for them. But, whereas these requirements are *imposed* on us — whether by an Authority we have freely elected to govern us and therefore actually representative of our own aggressiveness, or which we have been coerced into recognising and therefore not representative of our *particular* expression of greed, it is still an imposition by our lowest instincts — the loyalty and obedience required by a Master are freely accepted by the aspirant as a condition of his training and may be abandoned at any point where the aspirant wishes to finish his training; it is a requirement only so long as the aspirant places himself under the guidance and protection of that Master. Furthermore, although there is the pretence by our Authorities of welcoming criticism and of encouraging "discussion", the forms and channels of this criticism and discussion are so restricted as to render them ineffective; on the other hand, the requirement by a Master of literal acceptance of whatever he says is not with the object of making the aspirant his shadow and robbing him of initiative — it is the requirement of a doctor of his patient whose health and well being is the only reason for association, and it is the earnest wish of the Master that the aspirant use his initiative to the full to try to grasp the meaning and intention of the Master. The following story told me by a disciple of Meher Baba illustrates the compassion of the Master and his eagerness for his disciple's advancement.

"Once I was sitting with Baba and he said: 'I have all along been saying that I am One with everyone and everything. Have you grasped the meaning of it yet?' I answered that I hadn't. He said: 'Have you bestirred yourself, pricked your mind, to grasp it?' I replied I had but to no effect. 'So I have just accepted it, as I accept other things as your say and therefore true, and have left it at that.'

Baba replied, 'It is no good just "accepting" what I say — you must try to understand it. Use your whole mind and try to understand and you will.' "

158

It should also be remembered (see Note 19/11) that a real Master is one whose very existence among us is for the sole object of our well-being. Subscription of implicit obedience and unhesitatingly carrying out his orders can lead only out from self-entanglement into Self-knowledge. Obviously one is a fool of the most irresponsible order who offers such obedience to one who is not a Perfect Master. To the question how can one determine that someone is a Perfect Master may be answered, deserts are according to merits. The dishonest and the self-seeking will always pick the false teacher or the outright charlatan; the one who wants Truth MORE than anything else including himself will be led by his own *unexpressed* Truth to the man of Truth.

The same principle applies in life: one arrives at where one sets out for — the missile arrives at the target *at which* it was pointed.

29/6   *Islamic tradition:* in showing Jesus as less "remote" and more "human" than Christian tradition shows Him, Islamic tradition is more interesting than Christian. There is no reason why God should not have a sense of humour. In fact, if He hadn't, we couldn't — something cannot come from nowhere: every limited quality must come from an unlimited one. Meher Baba has said, "My sense of humour is Infinite." And where the Islamic tradition has an actual Koranic foundation or results from Mohammed's "Sayings", it will be truer than Christian, since the Koran was written by Jesus called by another name, and the Gospels weren't written by Jesus under any name, but by men long afterwards.

29/8   The reward for miracle-working amongst bigoted people is always violence — that is, when the "miracle-worker" does jobs on the grand scale, not just giving farmers rain or women babies, and especially when he claims divine authority. In the case of a Perfect Master like Shams, naturally he would know what the reward would be before he undertook the job — that is what is called compassion; in the case of Jesus, His miracles were a necessary part of His work which was crowned by His crucifixion with its attendant humiliation and was necessary for His work; as Mohammed's stoning was, and Meher Baba's bone-breaking was (and His final humiliation will be) necessary. Humiliation precedes Glory — Glory being the "effect" or "triumph" of the assertion of Unlimited Power under conditions of utter helplessness — the effect of the assertion of most Unlimitedness in most limitation. Compare with *The Little Flowers,* where Francis is said to be greater than Mary or the disciple John because his suffering had been greater. The looseness and stupidity of the statement that suffering is good for the soul will be apparent. Suffering, in itself, never was and never will be "good"— it is simply the attendant condition of unfoldment and true assertion. Every step in evolution must have been, and every step in unfoldment in a man is, attended by suffering and crowned by a minor "glory".

33/22   *"Let me be one day full fed, . . .":* said by Mohammed to God when God offered Him all riches that a man can desire.

33/24   *"I am as one . . . again":* said by Mohammed.

34/1   For the details of this period of Baba's work, see *The Wayfarers* by William Donkin, Meher Publications, Ahmednagar, India. This book is a magnificent piece of careful documentation. It is the only book of its kind in the English language or probably in any language, since there is no evidence of historical Avatar at any time having carried out such extensive work of this nature.

34/8   The conclusion of the Trojan war and the return of Odysseus and his men. For this section, see Odyssey.

34/11   *the Giant's cave:* the giant Polyphemus who killed and ate a number of Odysseus' companions when he put ashore on the island where Polyphemus lived, and whom Odysseus overcame and escaped by blinding him.

34/12   *Aeolus:* King of the "Islands of Music".

34/13   *Tantra:* a meditative method or practice in which the physical form of the desire which is to be mastered is itself used. Obviously its success depends on absolute honesty of purpose and obtaining a right guide in the matter; lack of these two requisites naturally leads to further enmeshment in the particular desire.

    Circe: a goddess who lived on another island where Odysseus put ashore, and by whose "wiles" Odysseus' men were turned into swine, but through whom Odysseus obtained mastery and "emerged gloriously".

34/14   *King Alcinous:* the ruler of the last island Odysseus reached, alone, and whose men carried Odysseus on his last stage to his native land in one night.

34/18   *Messenger:* Hermes, the messenger of the gods.

35/1   Refers to the subtle planes of consciousness which must be crossed on the way to Truth.

35/8   *Tukaram:* a Perfect Master in Maharashtra, India, in the seventeenth century. He explained once to his wife that the easiest way to get to God was to open the doors of one's house for anyone to take what he liked (to literally take no thought about tomorrow) and to continuously repeat the Name of God. She followed his advice, but on the second day, feeling extremely hungry, went to the temple and complained to Krishna who gave her some gold coins. On one occasion a farmer made a bargain with Tukaram that Tukaram might as well sit in the middle of his field of ripening wheat and do his repetitions of the Name of God and at the same time mind the birds, in return for which service the farmer would give him a portion of the harvest. Tukaram took the job on, and sitting on a raised seat repeated loudly all day the Name of God, and when the birds came, said to them, "Eat your fill little ones, for this food is provided for you by God, but you must not take any away with you." (You also must not provide for tomorrow.) When the farmer came and found there was no crop to harvest he hauled Tukaram to Court. Tukaram said he had only done what he had bargained to do — mind the birds! The Court adjourned to inspect the field, and lo! every ear was bursting with grain. The Court ruled that all grain over and above the field's average yield belonged to Tukaram. Tukaram quickly replied, "No, no! you cannot do that to me. I have had enough trouble from this business already, let alone having the fresh trouble of having all this wheat." To the reader who, while appreciating the Franciscan flavour of the situation, asks, "But how does a Tukaram eat? a man must either own or work or beg"— the answer is, he eats whatever is offered him for that day and accepts no provision. If nothing is offered, he does not eat. He never asks. This is the only true Christian position for any one who accepts Christ as his Master — unless he accepts begging as a discipline in humility as St. Francis did. For life of Tukaram and other Friends of God of this period, see the volumes of *Poet-Saints of Maharashtra,* translated by Justin E. Abbott. For those interested in the political background, see *The Grand Rebel* by Dennis Kincaid, Collins.

35/13   *Shamsuddin:* same as Shams-e-Tabriz.

35/15   *Odin:* in Norse mythology the King of the Gods. When the price of one of his eyes was demanded for knowledge, he paid it immediately.

35/16   *Kullervo:* one of the heroes in the Finnish epic *Kalevala.*

35/17   *Gorgon:* in Greek mythology a frightful creature, the sight of whom turned one into stone.

35/18   *Aias, Diomedes:* Greek heroes in the Trojan war.

        Bran: an early Irish hero who met his death fighting the sea.

35/19   *Achilles:* the greatest champion of the Greeks. It is strange that his withdrawal from the conflict is generally interpreted as "sulking" because King Agamemnon pinched his girl-friend, when in the context of Homer it is clearly a withdrawal of power by he who is bright, glorious.

35/21   *Hera:* Consort of Zeus.

        Fire: when the river Scamander, choked with the bodies of those who fell before Achilles, turned its waters against him and was threatening to overwhelm him, Hephaestus, the heavenly worker in metals and master of Fire, at the behest of Hera sent Fire against the River. See *Iliad* XXI.

35/29   *six ascending planes:* see *God Speaks* for detailed exposition.

36/18   *(I am as a man . . . rides on again):* said by Mohammed.

36/23   *(For it is mostly . . . love God):* intended in reference to love in its full and real sense. In its widest sense, all men love God — all men love someone, even if it is only themselves, and all ones including one's ownself-one is of, from, by and *is* God ("all songs are to Brahman"). It is, however, practically only in India that real lovers, i.e. ones who have literally and absolutely abandoned all for love, exist in this age.

36/29   *Now, God, as a man, . . . but suffered the roads to them:* compare the apparent lack of omniscience and the obvious non-use of it in Meher Baba's journeys (described in detail in *The Wayfarers*) with the apparently aimless wanderings and reasonless actions of Jesus according to the Gospels.

37/23   *Yellow Castle:* Chinese equivalent.

38/1   *Moinuddin Chishti:* a perfect master of the twelfth to thirteenth centuries.

160

38/6   *Nanak:* founder of the Sikh religion in the fifteenth century. On his passing, both Hindus and Moslems claimed his body. See *The Sikh Religion,* a translation of the Sikh Bible by M. A. Macauliffe, Oxford.

41/1   *Chargeman:* One who has the charge or real well-being of the people in an area. God functions, or Truth manifests, on each plane through the *form* of that plane. On the mental planes He manifests as the Divine Beloved — only the saints know what sort of a form that is! — on the subtle planes He manifests as Light, Music and Perfume; on the physical plane as a Perfect Man, a Perfect Master. The understanding of the being and the function of the Perfect Master renders Images, whether Christian or Hindu, unnecessary and shows prayer to an Absolute or Abstract God, as in Protestant Faiths, Christian or Hindu, to be absurd — as absurd as one standing with one's mouth open in a drought expecting water instead of going to a tap which is connected to a reservoir; or sitting in one's room at night making passes in the air for light instead of switching on current from a powerhouse.

The Perfect Master, in this figure, is the totality of water and power which feeds the reservoir and powerhouses of the saints and Chargemen. Hence it is said, "One moment in the company of a saint is equal to a hundred years of penances and prayers." And "one glance or touch from a Perfect Master can give one Realization" (permanent identity with God — as being no one but God, as being nothing other than Truth): an impossible pill for those who like playing "ostrich", but an amazing challenge to those who put Truth before dreams.

41/21   *Manasarowar:* a lake at the foot of Kailas peak. Literally, the Lake of the Mind. In Hindu mythology the lake over which the swan Hamsa (soul) circles gazing at its image in the water (see Note 19/1).

42/12   *Automedon:* one of the heroes in the *Iliad.*

42/33   *mastani:* female mast; *gitana:* gypsy. Mast is pronounced must; mastani, mustahnee.

42/34   *vina:* a stringed instrument having a very rich and subtle tone.

43/2   *Godavari's flood:* the river Godavari. There is an amusing angle to this incident. Waliji (which is an affectionate form of Wali, saint) was himself caught in the flood and had to wade through it to high ground!

43/6   *Vithoba:* a name of Krishna (God).

Pandharpur: one of the places beloved by the line of Maharashtra poet-saints and a place of great pilgrimage nowadays. It is said that long ago there lived at this spot a youth, Pundalik, who served his aged parents with perfect service. News of this reached Krishna, who, with a companion, came down from Heaven to see and enjoy this devotion. When they got near, the companion said to the youth, "See, Krishna Himself has come to visit you." The youth, tossing a brick towards them, answered, "Can't you see I'm busy with my parents — tell Him to stand on that till I've finished fixing them up." Krishna stood on the brick — and remains until this day standing there in the temple built around Him. As Meher Baba has often said, "I become the slave of My devotees."

43/31   *Chidambaram:* see *The Dance of Siva* and other works of A. K. Coomaraswamy. For list of his books, see Note 129/29.

43/32   *Agni-Hephaestus:* Agni (Sanskrit) Personification and power of fire; Hephaestus, see Note 35/21.

44/9   *City of Spirit:* see Chandogya Upanishad in the *Ten Principal Upanishads,* translated by Purohit Swami, Faber & Faber.

45/1   *Great Seclusion:* see account of this in *The Great Seclusion* by Ramjoo Abdulla and C. D. Deshmukh, M.A., Ph.D., London, Meher Publications, Ahmednagar, India.

49/29   *Junaid:* a Perfect Master in Arabia in the tenth century. He cited the obedience of Abraham, the patience of Job, the symbolism of Zacharias, the wearing of wool by Moses, the strangerhood of John (the Baptist), the homelessness of Jesus, and the poverty of Mohammed as being excellent attributes of Sufism and models for aspirants to seek to emulate. He also declared that spirituality was wholly "manner"— morals, in the real sense of the right relationship in every relation, the right (exactly correct) relationship with one's fellowmen and with God. See *Kashf al-Mahjub,* translated by R. A. Nicholson, Luzac & Co.

50/31   *threshold,... of old age:* the "Classical" Hindu life of a man is: Childhood,

161

Studentship, Householder, and at fifty years, Renunciation. The Sufis divide it into: 0-28, youth; 28-56, middle age; 56-84, old age.

54/34   *Isa:* Jesus.

55/4   *Achaian host:* the Greek Army.

55/21   *Majzoobiyat:* the state of consciousness at which *everyone,* whether "mast" or "salik", crazy or balanced, arrives, and in which the last vestige of falseness is wiped out and one is drowned in the Ocean of Truth, one's own true Being — either to remain in endless perfect identification, or rarely, to return *with* this identification unbroken to the world of men as a real servant of Humanity. See *God Speaks* for the exact details of all the various states of consciousness, including this.

Book II

62/10   *Abu Sa'id:* a Perfect Master in the eleventh century. He said, "During my novitiate there came a time when people clamoured to get sight of me and even followed me out into the country when I rode out. And one day a Voice said to me, 'Am I not enough?' Then later on, they despised me and from the gallery in the Mosque voided their filth on me. And again the Voice said to me, 'Am I not enough?' " He also said that one is not advanced on the Path until people hate one and drive one out as a madman. See *Studies in Islamic Mysticism* by R. A. Nicholson, Cambridge.

62/14   *"John the Miller grinds small, small, small —*
            The King's Son in Heaven pays for us all."
John Ball (fourteenth century). See *The Dream of John Ball* by William Morris.

63/5   *"When . . . Existenceknowledgebliss":* Sankaracharya.

Book III

76/37   *precious word:* a particular Name of God. In this "word" is contained the "treasure" which is the Master's gift to the disciple and which becomes revealed as the disciple's love for it grows. It must be remembered that, with rare exceptions, the disciple in the beginning is a mass of loves. He wants Truth, but he wants innumerable other wants as well. Devotion to this "precious word" and to the one who gives it to him gradually centres his heart on one love which is the Ground from which all his loves sprang. This devotion is the only true religion; and the unconscious appreciation of it is in all men and is behind all "singleness of purpose" in any field of action. Differences in singleness of devotion being only in object, was behind the master Jami's requirement of an aspirant that he must have wholeheartedly loved before coming to him for guidance.

78/4   *Odin:* see Note 35/15. For his thrusting the sword into a tree from which a youth, Sigmund, pulled it, after all the champions had failed, see *Volsunga Saga.*

78/13   *Annamayakosa:* gross body (the physical body); anna — food; maya — consisting of; kosa — sheath, case, shell, abode. *Pranamayakosa:* subtle body; prana — vital spirit, energy, power.

78/14   *Manasmayakosa:* mental body; manas — mind.
            Vigñana: discernment, knowledge.
            Ananda: bliss.

78/15   *Nirmanakaya:* begotten-body; nirman — measure, creating; kaya — body, appearance, person.

78/16   *Sambodhakaya:* knowledge-body; sambodha — knowledge.

78/17   *Dharmakaya:* truth-body; dharma — order, virtue essential quality.

Book IV

83/34   *Prometheus-Agni:* Prometheus, a Greek god who brought Fire down from heaven for men. This act is generally represented as being in defiance of Zeus and for which Zeus had him tortured. But when Prometheus is seen as an attribute of Zeus, who is the highest Being (God), as are all the other gods attributes, it is Zeus who suffers through Prometheus. For every gift from God there is a consequent suffering by Him.

86/16   More or less a direct "lift" from Hafiz.

87/21   *September:* readers in the Northern Hemisphere please remember that in the Southern Hemisphere the seasons are opposite. September is the beginning of Spring.

87/26   "Heresy is for the heretic
    And orthodoxy for the orthodox —
    But the dust of the rose-petal belongs to the perfume-seller."
                                                    — Attributed to Emperor Akbar.

Book V, Part I

91/26   Parvati as the loving Mother-aspect of God to Man.
91/29   equals Zarathustra.
91/30   equals Abraham.
91/32   equals Rama.
92/1   equals Krishna.
92/2   equals Buddha.
92/3   equals Jesus; Mohammed.
92/17   *Sita:* wife of Rama.
         Lakshman: brother of Rama.
92/19   *Hanuman:* chief disciple of Rama.
92/31   *Tansen:* a singer at the court of Akbar (sixteenth century).
92/37   *Qwaali:* the traditional singing of the Sufis (those who follow the Islamic esoteric method) in which the states of the lover in relation to the Beloved are expressed — the songs often using the texts of the great Sufi masters like Hafiz, or being paraphrases of them. This form of singing is still alive and flourishing in India, and even to a western ear, after a little acquaintance, is most appealing.
         Bhajan: songs in praise of God in His Avataric form — Hindu.
         Flamenco: traditional Spanish gypsy form of singing.
93/3   *Anuradhapura* is used throughout to designate the marvellous rendering of Buddha in stone at Anuradhapura, Ceylon.
93/4   *Hui Neng,* or Wei Lang: The thirty-third Patriarch of China in direct spiritual descent from Sakyamuni Buddha according to the Zen School. See *The Sutra of Wei Lang* (or Hui Neng), translated by Wong Mon-Lam, new edition by Christmas Humphreys, Luzac & Co., for The Buddhist Society, London.
93/5   *Zen:* a Japanese word derived through Chinese from Sanskrit Dhyana, meditation. Called by the Zen masters themselves, the Sudden Method, i.e. the method based upon absolute surrenderance and obedience to one's Master or spiritual guide. Zen, Sufism and Vedantism are really different "flavours" of this method.
93/7   *Shang:* the bright young man who tramped across China to meet Bodhidharma. After waiting outside in the snow for a week for an interview, sent in his right hand to show that he was really in earnest.
93/8   *Bodhidharma:* the Indian Master, the twenty-eighth in line from Buddha and the first Patriarch of China.
93/9   *Noh:* the traditional "classical" drama of Japan. See *"Noh" or Accomplishment,* by E. Fenollosa and Ezra Pound, Macmillan.
         tea drinking: The Book of Tea, by Okakura Kakuzo, Angus & Robertson.
93/11   *Thopaga:* "Great Sorcer", Guru Marpa's pet-name for Milarepa.
93/12   *Sankaracharya . . . "I am God":* Buddha, in His teaching, confined Himself to explaining only the Bliss aspect of Reality and said nothing about the Power, Knowledge aspects. Consequently, He explained the spiritual path only as far as Nirvana (passing away): that is, that which one takes to be "oneself"— that aggregate of impressions, the experiencing of which causes one to assert I am a man or a woman, rich or poor, strong or weak, bright or dull, and so forth — must pass away, must be annihilated. "Buddhism" took this "self" to mean Self (Paramatma, God) the Unborn the Undying One Existence without a second, and declared that Buddha taught that this Self had no existence.
Buddha, being this Self, could not possibly have taught that Self did not exist. That He chose to enlighten His disciples regarding the path only as far as Nirvana — which state is *inevitably* followed by Nirvikalpa (affirmation that "I am God") — is not our affair. The point is, the fact that a teacher, for reasons of his own, does

163

not include a particular aspect or further degree — in this case, a further state of consciousness — cannot in itself be taken as his denial of the existence of that aspect or degree. It was the mission of Sankaracharya to counteract this false teaching which was not Buddha's and which had bred a widespread atheism, and he had no hesitancy in revealing the facts of the ultimate Goal. In fact, Nirvikalpa or "I am God" state was the basis and conclusion of his teaching: Atma (individual self) *is* Paramatma (universal Self).

93/14   *Pragñanaparamitahridayasutra:* splits up into:
        pra-gña — intelligence, wisdom, knowledge;
        aparamita — limitless, measureless, infinite;
        hrid-aya — heart;
        sutra — a scripture, "a thread by which one is drawn along the path to Reality". The whole word might be rendered as, "the heart-doctrine, by practise of which, one obtains insight into the infinite." It is the name of one of the most important of the Mahayana (Great-vehicle) Buddhist texts. It is included in the Evans-Wentz series. See Note 27/8.

93/18   See *The Desert Fathers,* by Helen Waddell, Constable.

93/19   See *The Seven Odes,* translated by A. J. Arberry, George Allen & Unwin. Other books by Arberry are: *Kings and Beggars* (Sadi's Gulistan), Luzac & Co.; *The Koran Interpreted* (The Koran), Allen & Unwin; *The Quatrains of Baba Tahir,* Emery Walker Ltd.

93/20   *Kailas frescoes:* at Ellura, near Aurangabad, Deccan, India, there are some thirty man-made caves filled with Buddhist, Jain and Saivite sculpture. The glory of them all is a complete and large temple cut into the hillside of solid stone. There is no portion of it where stone has been laid on stone, it is all cut out of the one body of stone. On its walls and on the walls of the "galleries" flanking it the life-story of Siva has been cut. The general plan or shape of it is modelled on the shape of Mt. Kailas. This, together with it being the Abode of Siva, gives it its name, Kailas Temple.
        Jesus, Sun of fourth heaven: see *Mathnawi.*

93/25   *Abu Bakr:* Chargeman of Mohammed in the sense as Peter was of Jesus.
        Ali: the third in line from Mohammed.
        Ibn 'Arabi, Attar, Abu Sa'id: Sufi Masters. For Attar, see *Attar,* by Margaret Smith, "Wisdom of the East Series", and *The Conference of the Birds,* by S. C. Nott, Janus Press.

93/27   *Chretien de Troyes* is published in "Everyman's Library". For Daniel, see *The Spirit of Romance,* by Ezra Pound, Peter Owen.
        Ramon Lull: his *Blanquerna* is translated by E. Allison Peers, Jarrolds.

94/9   *Khizr:* in the Sufi tradition, a timeless "Person", Keeper of the Waters of Knowledge, who appears to special devotees throughout the ages. The Master of Moses. See *Islamic Mysticism* and *Kashf Al-Mahjub.*

94/14   *Demodocus:* the blind bard at the Court of King Alcinous.

95/22   *"Your pride . . .":* Vivekananda.

95/27   See *The Holy Mountain.*

96/4   *"Without the Name . . .":* Inayat Khan.

96/9   *Sheik Abu'l Fadl:* the Master of Abu Sa'id.

96/17   *Patanjali:* see *Yoga, Aphorisms of,* translated by Purohit Swami, Faber & Faber.

97/28   *Majnun and Leila:* the classical Persian lovers.

97/35   *Eknath:* see the vol. *Eknath* in "Poets Saints of Maharashtra". See Note 35/8.

97/37   *Advaita:* "One without a second".

98/6   *Sankirtan:* a recital of the qualities of God, generally with musical accompaniment.

100/24   *Adamic:* Fabre d'Olivet in his *The Hebraic Tongue Restored,* Putnam & Sons, renders Eve as the "volative faculty", the "intellectual companion" of Adam.

101/15   *Ares:* the Greek god of war.

102/27   *Picasso:* the greatest living European painter.

102/28   *Eliot, T. S.:* the most representative poet of the present peculiar English mentality which is the result of declining material power without any spiritual basis upon which to rest and re-grow from.

102/29   *Obey:* a French play-writer.

164

102/31   *Fry:* an English play-writer.
102/33   *I. Khan:* Inayat Khan. See Note 129/26.
103/11   *Master Kung:* Confucius (sixth century B.C.). See translations of his works by Arthur Waley and by Ezra Pound.
103/13   *Laotze:* his single work is translated by Waley under the title of *The Way and its Power,* Allen & Unwin. For incident quoted, see *Master Kung,* by Carl Crow, Hamish Hamilton.
104/23   *John:* St. John of the Cross.
104/27   *"No Guru no Shishya":* "(I am) neither teacher nor pupil". Sankaracharya in his Nirvan Shatak.

Book V, Part II

110/13   *"blank-paper scripture":* in the delightful Chinese novel, *Monkey,* translated by Arthur Waley, Allen & Unwin, Tripitaka arrives, after a most hazardous and adventurous journey, at the Monastery and is given a scroll of the True Scripture. When he opens it he finds it is only blank paper. Upon his complaint about this, he is told that that is the True Scripture, but if he wants some with writing he can have those too.
110/29   *Guernica:* a large painting by Picasso depicting the destruction of a world. Siva-Bhairav — a representation in the temple of Kailas at Ellura of Siva as Destroyer. Apart from the contrast of these two works in isolation, the difference is even more marked in context — Guernica in the context of Picasso's body of work, and the Bhairav in the context of the whole series of sculpture depicting the life-story of Siva.
111/8   *David:* an Old Testament master.
111/10   *Solomon:* an Old Testament master; *Namdev:* a Maharashtrian poet-saint.
111/11   *Enoch:* an Old Testament master.
111/13   *"five prayers":* Mohammed was asked by the people how often they should pray. Mohammed referred the matter to God, who answered, "Continuously." The people said, "Doesn't He know that we have work to do!" (or something like that). God brought it down to forty times a day. "Nothing doing," they said. "There wouldn't be enough time left between prayers to scramble a living." It was reduced to ten, to five, but they still complained. Below five God would not come, so five times a day it is for all Moslems *and* Mohammedans.
111/29   *Ezra Pound:* the greatest writer in English in this century. The only pity is that he hasn't written in English more.
111/32   *Bullah Shah:* as a child he was very backward. By the time the other children had mastered the Arabic alphabet, he hadn't learned the first letter. His parents took him away from school and left him to himself. He ran away to the desert or jungle or whatever sort of country it was out from the town and spent his whole time in trying to understand the meaning of this single letter "a" which also stands for the number "one". After twenty-five years he returned to his childhood school and took his place in the class he had left. The same teacher, an old man now, asked him what he wanted. He said he had come for his second lesson. To humour this madman the teacher asked him to write his first lesson on the blackboard. He did so; and the whole wall split in two.
115/37   *Little Preludes of John Sebastian Bach:* Bach was not only one of the greatest European Music-masters, but also seems to have been an ideal teacher of children and wrote a quantity of graded pieces, beginning with L.P., for them.
117/27-28   For *Paul, Anthony, Bemus, Theon, Macarius, Hyperichas, Achilles and Paphnutius,* see *The Desert Fathers,* by Helen Waddell, Constable.
        For *Hrut, Kari, Flosi, Njal and Bergthore,* see *Njal-Saga.*
        For *Isidore,* see *Saints and Saint Makers of New Mexico,* by E. Boyd, Laboratory of Anthropology, Sante Fe, New Mexico.
117/34   *Lu:* one of the ancient Prophet-Kings of China.
118/1   *Tai Shan:* a holy mountain in China; *Meru:* same as Kailas.
118/8   *Bhanudas:* see the vol. *Bhanudas* in "Poet-Saints of Maharashtra".

Book V, Part III

123/12   *Andromache:* wife of Hector, the greatest champion among the Trojans.
123/13   *Pelides:* Achilles.
123/14   *Thetis:* mother of Achilles.
124/20   *"Where is ... me?": Illuminations* by Arthur Rimbaud.
124/23   *"God made ... himself":* Katha Upanishad. See *Ten Principal Upanishads.*
129/25   *Vivekananda:* the great disciple of Ramakrishna Paramhamsa. Went to the West first in 1898. Works obtainable from any of the Ramakrishna Missions, Headquarters, Belur Math, Calcutta.

                Coomaraswamy, A. K.: Works include, *The Dance of Siva,* The Sunwise Turn, New York; *Am I My Brother's Keeper,* The John Day Co., New York; *Transformation of Nature in Art,* Harvard University Press; *The Mirror of Gesture,* E. Weyhe, New York; (with Sister Nivedita) *Myths of the Hindus and Buddhists,* Holt & Co., New York.

129/26   *Inayat Khan:* went to U.S.A. in 1910 as a musician. Later settled in Paris as a teacher of Sufi Philosophy. Works published by Kluwer, Deventer, Holland.

Book V, Part IV

141/1   *Prajapati:* as the First teacher of Man is the same as Siva or Adi Buddha.
                Manu: an ancient Law-giver. See *The Laws of Manu,* "Sacred Books of the East", ed. Max Muller, Oxford.
141/8   *Fenollosa:* see his *Epochs of Chinese and Japanese Art,* Heinemann.
141/10   *"Santos":* Saints and Saintmakers of New Mexico, see Note 117/27.
142/21   *Gunnar:* the greatest champion of Iceland. See *Njal Saga.*
145/27   *avidya:* ignorance; *one lakh:* 100,000.
146/24   *"Yer know ... right!":* Kabir.
146/27   *"one hour ... fighter":* Arsenius. See *The Desert Fathers.*
146/34   *"Cunning ... performance":* one of Confucius' disciples came upon a man watering his garden from a well by means of a pitcher. He told the gardener that there *was* an improved method of irrigation, to which he replied that he had heard of such things but his Master had always taught him (as above), and thereby one loses the purity of one's heart.
149/17   *"O God! O God!":* the prayer of Francis of Assisi.
150/8   See the *Agamemnon* of Aeschylus.
150/37   *Sigurd:* the greatest of the Norse heroes. See *Volsunga Saga.*
152/12   *Ganesh:* power; *surya:* the Sun; *Saraswati:* the goddess of learning.

166

Dreaming and Dreaming

When you sleep and dream you experience association with people, speaking with them and doing actions in relation to them, see all manner of objects in your surroundings, and feel happiness or unhappiness in regard to them all. Where do all these people and objects come from? Not from outside yourself but from within you. You create them for your own experiencing—and *no one but you* sees, knows about and experiences what you are seeing, knowing and experiencing. They exist only for you.

In like manner, you are sitting in this room seeing these other persons and the objects in the room, and, in like manner, *no one but you* is seeing them and experiencing them—that is, seeing and experiencing them as *you* are seeing and experiencing them. They exist solely for you and have come from nowhere but from within you — you have created them for your experience of them.

What is called your "awake-state", your daily life with all its associations and experiences is only you dreaming and in your dream creating all the persons and objects in that dreaming for your experience of them; what is called your dreaming when asleep is but another dream within this dream.

When you awake from your asleep-dreaming into your awake dream you know that the asleep-dreaming *was* only a dream. When you awake from your awake-dreaming you will know that you were the sole creator of both the dreams, and all the people, objects and situations contained in them — that they existed only in you and were for *no one but you* and were nothing but dream experiences of your own dreaming; and that you alone have Real Existence.

WHEN REAL LIGHT APPEARS
THIS DARKNESS
WHICH YOU THINK IS LIGHT
DISAPPEARS.

MEHER BABA